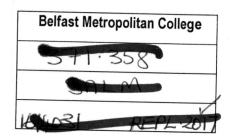

D0230717

E-tivities

The world of learning and teaching is at a watershed; confronted by challenges to previous educational models. One learning future lies in impactful, purposeful, active online activities, or 'e-tivities', that keep learners engaged, motivated and participating. Grounded in the author's action research, *E-tivities, 2nd edition* assuredly illustrates how technologies shape and enhance learning and teaching journeys.

In this highly practical book, Gilly Salmon maintains her exceptional reputation, delivering another powerful guide for academics, teaching professionals, trainers, designers and developers in all disciplines. This popular text has been comprehensively updated; addressing key technological changes since 2002, offering fresh case studies and 'Carpe Diem'—a unique approach to learning design workshops.

Readers will find *E-tivities, 2nd edition* a wonderful resource on its own or as a companion to the author's bestselling *E-moderating, 3rd edition.*

Find e-tivities on the Web at e-tivities.com or connect at gillysalmon.com.

Professor Gilly Salmon is Pro Vice-Chancellor of Learning Transformations at Swinburne University of Technology, Australia.

E-tivities

The Key to Active Online Learning

Second Edition

GILLY SALMON

 Routledge
Taylor & Francis Group

NEW YORK AND LONDON

First published 2013
by Routledge
711 Third Avenue, New York, NY 10017

Simultaneously published in the UK
by Routledge
2 Park Square, Milton Park, Abingdon, Oxon OX14 4RN

Routledge is an imprint of the Taylor & Francis Group, an informa business

© 2013 Taylor & Francis

Library of Congress Cataloguing in Publication Data
Salmon, Gilly.
    E-tivities: the key to active online learning/by Gilly Salmon.
    —Second edition.
    pages cm
    Includes bibliographical references and index.
    1. Teaching—Computer network resources.   2. Computer-assisted
    instruction.   3. Distance education.   I. Title.
    LB1044.87.S25 2014
    371.33′4—dc23
    2013000706

ISBN: 978-0-415-88175-3 (hbk)
ISBN: 978-0-415-88176-0 (pbk)
ISBN: 978-0-203-07464-0 (ebk)

Typeset in Bembo and Gill Sans
by Florence Production Ltd, Stoodleigh, Devon, UK

Printed and bound in Great Britain by
TJ International Ltd, Padstow, Cornwall

For Sophia

Contents

Foreword

I am delighted that Gilly Salmon has decided to update this important book, which, along with its highly successful companion *E-moderating,* has done so much to improve the practice of e-learning and render it enjoyable for both learners and teachers. With forecasts suggesting that 80 per cent of US students will be taking courses online in 2014, along with the rest of the world going down the same track, this new edition is very timely.

Online learning was in its infancy in most institutions when the first edition was published in 2002. The most common model for producing e-learning courses was that individual academics created online versions of their regular classroom offerings—with as much or as little help as their institution saw fit to provide. Tony Bates called this the 'Lone Ranger' model and argued that it was unlikely to produce consistent quality at the course level, or coherent programmes.

Since those days online learning has achieved much greater maturity. Realizing the importance of online teaching to their future strategies, institutional leaders are now providing more effective frameworks for course development and student support.

Meanwhile, technology marches on. The first edition of *E-tivities* was published in the same year as United Nations Educational Scientific and Cultural Organization (UNESCO) held the forum that coined the term 'open educational resources' (OER). The subsequent decade has seen the burgeoning of OER worldwide and the development of increasingly powerful tools for locating OER of relevance to a particular course. Today, creating online courses is more about finding and adapting good OER than developing original content from scratch.

At the same time, the social media have strongly reinforced the role of inter-activity in online learning—what was called 'computer-mediated conferencing' at the time of the first edition.

These changes have combined to lead teachers to take naturally to the ideas of learning design, something that few bothered with a decade back. This new edition of *E-tivities* feeds that trend perfectly. It is easy to say that the Lone Ranger method of course development should give way to a team approach—less easy to show staff how to take that on. Gilly Salmon has a spent a decade researching and testing approaches to make this transition both productive and enjoyable.

These results are presented in Chapter 5 in particular, where the Latin term *carpe diem* (seize the day) captures the idea that every moment of the time that teams are being trained together should be spent on designing something that could be put into immediate use with participants. With this technique, developing learning with technology is no longer a 'solo' activity but rather a design and 'ecological' experience.

The name of Gilly Salmon has become synonymous with effective, exciting and interactive e-learning. I am delighted that she has taken the trouble to share her most recent thinking and experience in this book and I commend it to a wide readership.

Sir John Daniel
28 January 2013

Preface to the second edition

This revision of *E-tivities* comes 10 years after its first publication in 2002. So much has happened in that period: thousands of e-tivities have been planned, executed and experienced by the growing worldwide army of online designers, learning technologists, e-moderators, researchers, commentators—and, of course, online learners.

Today, new learners, young, old and in between, are connected at the speed of light. Every individual is a node on a learning network. We can call them the Quantum Generation: they are making a quantum leap into an increasingly complex digital world. Most importantly, we finally need to acknowledge that *we are not trying to replicate the class or lecture room 'learning' experience of old. We can do it better. We've been far too coy about this to date.*

In the introduction to her book *Hamlet on the Holodeck: The Future of Narrative in Cyberspace*, Janet Murray (Murray, 1997) made the case that online literature promises us the very things and experiences that are essential to print-based literature, but in more intensified and more accessible ways. For Murray, hypertext, cyberdrama and the 'literature' of new technologies are not something radically at odds with print-based texts and culture—but rather an extension. She writes:

> I am not among those eager for the death of the book . . . Nor do I fear it as an imminent event. The computer is not the enemy of the book. It

is the child of print culture, a result of the five centuries of organized, collective inquiry and invention that the printing press made possible.

(Murray, 1997, p. 8)

Over the past 10 years, as I've seen the truly enormous struggle to make the very best of new technologies and the transformation in learning that they can bring, I've often thought of this insight. I've had the privilege to watch—and indeed be part of—the yearly growth in commitment to ingenuity in learning among teachers and students fired by the availability of networking computing . . . a great creative wellspring of our special time. The media we now use, adapt and yearn for reflects opportunities for fresh types of expression, innovative forms of contributions and, yes, a revolution in the nature of knowledge itself. Murray pointed out that the personal computer promised to reshape knowledge in ways that sometimes complement and sometimes supersede the work of the book and the lecture hall (pp. 9–10). I like to think that the branches that I call e-tivities are making a positive and successful impact to new genres for learning.

If I have stimulated, cajoled or prompted people to make this quantum leap, or sometimes absolutely insisted that they do so, then I am both proud and extremely pleased. There's been much joy. But I also hold that this growing base of people, activities and experiences has not yet reached critical mass. So I felt compelled to write this second edition. The designers, dispensers and pedlars of online pedagogy have much more impact yet to make, through the principles and practices expressed in this book, if we are to make our full contribution to learning and teaching in the rather extraordinary second decade of the twenty-first century . . . and beyond.

So, no pressure then!

Let me take stock of—and paraphrase—what has happened in the world of learning and teaching in the last 10 years, because they explain why I think e-tivities are the key to the future success of active and interactive online learning.

In 2002, when the first edition of *E-tivities* was published, only around 40 per cent of educational institutions in developed countries had an online learning platform, that is, a learning management system, or virtual learning environment (LMS/VLE in this book). That year, one of today's popular platforms (Moodle) was first released. As I write, the latest version of the Moodle LMS/VLE exists and operates in 70,793 registered or verified sites, serving a staggering 63.2 million users in over 6.7 million courses overseen by in excess of 1.2 million teachers. There are many other popular platforms and products being extensively put to work as well. Almost every institution around the world has a LMS/VLE and many are on their second or third product. Many are now adding a wide variety of mobile and social media options, too—ones that they are never going to actually own. Another quantum leap! So, an important substrate or technological capability layer on which e-tivities can be delivered and sustained has become ubiquitous during the last 10 years.

In 1994, the world's crude birth rate was determined to be around 21 births per year per 1,000 head of global population (www.index.mundi.com), when the world population was around 6 billion (www.prb.org). About 126 million people might have survived to reach the age of post-school education entry somewhere on the planet by 2012. Let's just consider higher education for a start. Each of the estimated 9,000 universities around the world would have to absorb a 'fresher' intake of around 14,000 students this year, and continue to do that in the coming years, to satisfy this need. Incidentally, more and more people are reaching the end of their compulsory schooling with the qualifications they need for further study. Most institutions in most countries do not have campuses, facilities or estates lying idle. Most colleges and universities typically take between 1,000 and 7,000 new students each year to optimize their capacity and make their learning businesses financially viable.

The world simply cannot provide the traditional campus-based experience to meet such a demand (see, for example, www.col.org/resources/speeches/pages). We can neither afford to build the extra physical facilities needed nor build that capacity fast enough to meet the extra demand. So, a 1,000-year-old model—in which those who wanted education and enlightenment, and could afford to do so, physically travelled to seats or centres of learning to be taught by, and to study under, the best and most knowledgeable academic minds—no longer has the infrastructure, resources and growth investment to meet and satisfy its 21st-century quantum market.

The answer—or part of it, anyway—to this problem lies in different modes of presentation and delivery of teaching and learning opportunities. Digital approaches can turn that 1,000-year-old model on its head: if the student cannot come to the institution, then the institution must reach out to the student. And why not, in doing so, and make education better, too? It can be done with relatively no cost and high value for learning technologies. Digitally enhanced course design, for globally connected and distributed communities of learners, requires e-tivities in paced and scheduled programmes. They are not lectures, they are not massive open online courses (MOOCs), but they are scalable and easy to do. Many small e-tivities add up to a quantum leap in learning and teaching experiences.

Ubiquitous, reliable, robust, capable and consumer-orientated technologies such as laptops, wireless connectivity and smart phones have been adopted and adapted by education. Once that marketplace's potential was recognized, other enabling technology developers and suppliers crowded the space with further products—and then fought a battle of price sensitivity and attractiveness with each other to secure their share of that vast, constantly changing and hugely lucrative market. Choice was never as rich as it is now, and never was capability and the rate of advance of those technology parameters as high as it is right now. This inexorable march of technology and its adoption by a globally connected consumer society has simply rendered less distinctive—and more permeable—the differences between one kind of consumer and the next. Today both undergraduates and CEOs carry a smart phone—both access the vast resources of the Internet in their daily lives and their devices never leave their sides. Extraordinarily rapidly, we have become used to the notion that you can easily and cheaply deliver messages, information, data or learning materials to someone via the connectivity that that person's device enjoys, pretty much wherever they may be at any time. As a result, our social world and the ways we live our lives are transformed.

So, given that these mature and low-cost technologies can return such a bang for each buck, we have a really marvellous and amazing opportunity to embrace and exploit them to the fullest; to advance and expand the degree, extent and reach of our educational provisions and deliver that opportunity to all. Why not engage the middle manager or corporate director in the acquisition of a Masters in Business Administration (MBA) via his smart phone, tablet and/or home and office laptop or iPad whilst he or she continues to realize the strategic goals of the corporation? Why not provide the budding scientist with brilliant new ways of understanding concepts? Why not use technologies to reach new customers for education, new markets for learning on the move, to render borders and boundaries, geographic location and access as irrelevant? And why not do it using and creating quantum knowledge?

The reason 'why not' is that we do not have 1,000 years of tradition to draw on. Our educational institutions are simply not structured for rapid change. There have been many failures of e-learning initiatives to date simply because the only learning design that is truly known and embedded is based on campus approaches. A rethink is required, a recreation of viable and preferred ways. Luckily there are now few constraints that—with technology as our partner and pedagogical ally—we cannot overcome to reach out and offer, like never before, the opportunity of an innovative educational experience that once would have been considered impossible or impracticable.

Since 2002, initiatives and policies aimed at increasing that proportion of the population entitled to go beyond formal school education, whilst simultaneously shifting much of the funding and cost of that experience from the state to individual students (over their working lives), have transformed what students expect.

Our future learners will continue to be those generations born into an ever more technologically and infrastructurally enriched world. Furthermore, the digital world and all its learning benefits cross and embrace all generations and wealth divides. The newer entrants will have known, experienced and become adept at using those technologies almost from birth, and will have unimaginable opportunities for true life-long learning. They will know less about any other older forms of information, knowledge and learning access and acquisition and be less indentured to or inclined to pursue those more antique and improbable ways. They will be more mobile than any generation before them and they will be simultaneously much more connected, available and communicable. The notion of a learning experience that dominates and influences where you live during that experience will not be something that the Quantum Generation holds to be valid.

Consumer expectations will be changed by having a university education that students subsequently pay for over the working life that their degrees have enabled them to have. This will introduce the belief amongst many students that, if they have to pay for it, then they might as well study while they work to pay off the cost of the experience. There will be a growth in part-time and work-located forms of study, both of which require connectivity and delivery to a remote or distant location rather than a campus and which may also require some interesting but not impossible to solve technology discussions with employers, corporations and companies. Investment in more campus-based teaching and learning capacity and buildings is only going to work for those institutions that consistently turn away two or more applicants for every graduate place that they offer whilst still fulfilling their government quotas and standards. There will instead be a huge shift, from using students' previous attainments as proxy for quality, to having to teach much better, and much more appropriately. For every other institution the future lies in delivering learning and teaching to remote and changing consumer locations, defined by where students are currently connected.

How can we solve or respond to this conundrum, no, this challenge? Surely a significant part of the answer lies in a shift towards a quality, achievable digital-first online delivery, new design, online collaborative tasks, online assignments, online student educational experiences—and that's what e-tivities can stimulate, encourage, support and make happen.

Have I begun to convince you of how different the world of learning is about to become, and how valid and valuable your understanding and adoption of the principles embedded in this book are going to be?

Read on—and enjoy! You can read the book in sequence or dip in and out. The book is in two main parts: e-tivities explanations in Part I and more (I hope) inspiration and practical stuff in Part II. Just check out the 'Invitational' framework on the next few pages first, please. Don't forget to explore the e-tivities footprint on the Web through e-tivities.com and gillysalmon.com for community updates. This is how we shape the future. Be part of the Quantum Generation of learning design.

Gilly Salmon
Melbourne
January 2013

Acknowledgements

The research and practice for this second edition of the *E-tivities* book has spanned 10 very happy and productive years, during which time I have worked at two UK and two Australian universities. I was at the Open University Business School until 2004 and at the University of Leicester until 2010. For the past two years at I have worked in Australia: at the University of Southern Queensland in Toowoomba and now at Swinburne University of Technology in Melbourne. Each university in its own special way has not only given me space, resources, people and encouragement to develop and understand e-tivities and the five-stage model but also a cast of thousands, staff and students, who have listened, influenced, practised and contributed to the development of understandings of how to embed the models and frameworks.

Thanks go to the senior executive and management of each university for their support and encouragement, and their recognition of the importance of creating the future through learning design, but most of all to my colleagues in each place and time for their extraordinary tolerance, support and feedback.

Outside the four universities, special thanks and acknowledgements also go to communities of knowledge building, understanding and practice for their constant impacts—the 'Follow the Sun' conference developers and delegates, the Association of Learning Technologies (ALT) and the UK Higher Education Academy. I asked for help from the ALT community for the technology chapter (Chapter 4) and got it from Jo Axe, Chiara Balasubramaniam, Dawne Bell, Jane Brotchie, Sarah Chesney, Sharon Gardner, Darren Gash, Doug Gowan, Peter Hartley, Oriel Kelly, Emma King, Lesley Pyke, Daniel Scott and Thomas Wanner.

Swinburne Online is a joint venture with Swinburne University and SEEK Limited (www.seek.com.au). I'm delighted to see that they have fully embraced the notions of the five-stage model, e-moderating and e-tivities. As I write, Swinburne Online has been admitting students through this new digitally engaged and high-quality regime for fewer than 12 months, to great success. It's great for e-tivities to be scaled up in this way, but mostly the thanks go to the amazing people who have made it happen, the e-moderators (called e-learning advisors by Swinburne Online) and of course their participants. You will see their influence and comments throughout this book. Especial thanks go to Denice Pitt, Kay Lipson and Sue Kokonis and to all the Swinburne Online Learning Designers and the 'Duet' academics who transferred their knowledge. Thanks to some of the first students from Swinburne Online who gave their feedback, including Helen Cameron, Greg Cowlishaw, Rosalie Dyson, Belinda Hartney, Danielle Payne and Debra Stephenson.

The e-moderating and e-tivities course through All Things in Moderation (www.atimod.com) were the first test-beds and development opportunities for e-tivities and you will see quotes throughout the book. Endless thanks go to David Shepherd and Ken Giles for their patient e-moderating of the many online courses that introduced e-tivities in an accessible and usable way to many individuals and groups. Many thanks for the faith and commitment of all the first-time e-moderators and e-tivities designers, many of whom have gone on to influence learning design in a very wide variety of spheres, sectors and disciplines. Social media is gradually bringing us back together to share further knowledge, so don't forget to check out the Facebook site (www.facebook.com/GillySalmonOnlineLearning).

The original e-tivities research was carried out whilst I was working at the Open University Business School in the UK, one of the largest and greatest open pedagogical engines in the world. I was most fortunate to have such an environment in which to learn, teach and research (with study leave) in the 'early days' of online study.

Lots of different people contributed to the development and evolution of the Carpe Diem process, from its very early days and roots in Glasgow to the current branches, diffusion and expansion in many different places. You can read about it in Chapter 5. Especial mention to those at the University of Leicester including Alejandro Armellini, Simon Kear, Gabi Witthaus, Terese Bird and all the Media Zoo project people and partner academics for their commitment and contributions. Thanks especially to Catriona Burke and team at Kemmy Business School, Limerick; Sharmini Thurairasa and team at Swinburne University of Technology, Melbourne; Shirley Reushle and team at the University of Southern Queensland and Simon Kear now at Goldsmiths London. You can read their stories and case studies in Chapter 5.

Thanks to Nell Bong-Jensens who most freely offered advice on cross-cultural names for our learner in the sketches of 'Mo'. Thanks also to Mark Tayar for help with sourcing information for updating Resources for Practitioners 16 to support learners with disabilities.

My support at Swinburne University includes the extraordinary work and contribution from Janet Gregory, who was Swinburne's first official trainee Carpe Diem facilitator and got very successful e-moderating courses off the ground very quickly. She even insists she enjoyed it. Ben Mackenzie has worked tirelessly and effectively to get the concepts of active online learning effectively transferred to Swinburne Online, through a process we call 'Duet'. Derek Whitehead and colleagues from the library at Swinburne are so helpful in exploring the brave new world of digital resources.

Professor David Hawkridge of the Open University and the University of Leicester has once again patiently and speedily offered his unending wisdom and advice on my maybe over-enthusiastic writing. Phemie Wright has worked with me as researcher and project helper throughout the development of this second edition of *E-tivities*. This book simply would not have happened without her insights and hard work. Thanks to both of these people who in their own quiet ways have hugely impacted on the world of e-tivities.

Rod Angood drew the pictures. You can find them in colour on e-tivities.com and visiondirecting.com.

Throughout the development and writing I have learned from and been encouraged by my fully digitally connected family, Rod, Glenn, Emily and Paula. Love and thanks, everyone. A special mention to my new granddaughter, Sophia Kate Lily, born in August 2012, to whom this book is dedicated. She can already Skype.

Note on use of shaded text

Throughout this book, I use real online messages from courses that I design or run as illustrations. I indicate a screen message by shading, as in this paragraph. Messages have had to be pruned to reduce the amount of space they take up in the book, but I have not attempted to correct their grammar or informal language. By the way, looking at selected messages in print after the interactive event makes them seem more organized than they really were. Live e-tivities are likely to be messier!

(All e-tivities images by Rod Angood at www.visiondirecting.com)

Part 1:
INTRODUCING E-TIVITIES

Table 1.1 E-tivity framework: the invitation

Numbering, sequencing, pacing
Title
Purpose
Task summary
Spark
Individual contribution
Dialogue begins
E-moderator interventions
Schedule and time
Next

Table 1.2 E-tivity framework: how to create an invitation

Numbering, pacing and sequencing	*Number as follows: week.sequence of task (e.g. 2.4 would be week 2, task 4)*
Title	• Enticement to open the invitation to take part. • Very brief descriptor. • Be inventive and creative, but keep it very short.
Purpose	• Explain. If you complete this activity, you will be able to . . . • You will understand better how to . . . • You will find it essential for assignment X . . . • Use verbs! • Link directly with your outcomes and/or objectives for the unit, module, course and programme.
Brief summary of overall task	• If you find you have more than one major activity or question, divide into more e-tivities. • Clear, brief instructions on how to take part and what to do. • One question or task per message. • When you have written this part, check that the task is self-contained.
Spark	• Spark to light the fire for the topic, interesting little intervention. • Directly link with topic for this week. • Opportunity to expose 'content' but with the purpose of a spark to start a dialogue with others.
Individual contribution	• Give clear instructions to the individual participant as to what he or she should do in response to the spark. • Specify exactly what you are expecting the participant to do and in what media (e.g. wiki, discussion board, audio file, etc.) and by when (i.e. the day and date). Tell them the length of contribution expected. • Create a link from this part of the invitation to the location for posting.
Dialogue begins	• Request response from an individual to others, what kind of response, how long, where and by when. • Key point: students come online to see if others have read and responded. Make this happen. • Create a link from this part of the invitation to the location for posting the response to others.
E-moderator interventions	• Clearly indicate what the e-moderator will do and when. • Explain that the e-moderator will summarize, give feedback and teaching points and close the e-tivity, and when this will happen.
Schedule and time	• Total calendar/elapsed time allowed for this e-tivity. • Completion date. • Estimate total study time required (e.g. 2 x 1 hour).
Next	• Link to next e-tivity. • You can suggest additional resources to help with the task—indicate whether they are required or optional, place the links at the end of the invitation.

Chapter 1

E-tivities for active online learning

You can bask in the glory of happy, engaged and achieving online students. This book explains and explores e-tivities, the name I give to frameworks for enabling active and participative online learning by individuals and groups. E-tivities are important for the online teaching and learning world because they deploy useful, well-rehearsed principles and pedagogies for learning as well as your choice of networked technologies.

E-tivities do not remove the help and input of more knowledgeable humans—the people I called the 'e-moderators'—but make their work more focused and productive. They focus on the learners—the people I call the participants, who are contributing, providing, reworking, interpreting, combining most of the knowledge. They overturn the idea that learning depends on one big expert and his/her conveying of knowledge.

E-tivities enable enjoyable and productive online learning for the greatest number of participants at the lowest cost. E-tivities are highly scalable. They are based on the strong idea that knowledge is constructed by learners through and with others. Such processes can happen through online environments just as well as in physical or formal learning and teaching environments, probably better. They work well combined with real-life and real-world environments.

You will find here the original e-tivities research and the learning that has emerged from extensive and intensive 12 years of practice, so you can design and deliver e-tivities for yourself—easily, quickly and effectively.

E-tivities were first developed using text-based computer-mediated environments such as bulletin boards or forums. That's the easiest place to start. I go on to describe how to use them for many other platforms. Once you get the idea, you will be able to use them in many different ways.

Learning resources and materials (what people once called 'content') are involved in the design and delivery of e-tivities, but these are to provide a stimulus or a start (the 'spark') to the interaction and participation rather than as the focus of the activity. So e-tivities give us the final break point from the time-consuming 'writing' of online courses.

Introducing e-tivities

The boxes below give you a quick introduction to e-tivities: who they're for, what they can be, where they are valuable, what their purposes are and what you need to produce them.

E-tivities are for:

- at least two people working and learning together in some way, and usually many more;
- participants who are not in the same locations. But e-tivities are also easily combined with location-based learning and teaching activities;
- a wide range of people, including those with disabilities who can be assisted through the technologies. The more diverse, the better the e-tivities work;
- everyone: e-tivities have attracted the interest of learning designers, academics, teachers and trainers from many sectors and levels of education.

E-tivities are:

- designed in advance of the participants' online arrival;
- quick and easy to produce, making the work of the tutor, or the person I call the e-moderator, much faster, easier and more productive;
- suitable for entirely online programmes, for integrated and blended learning, mobile learning and everything in between;
- cheap to create and run;
- scalable and customizable;
- efficient for designers, participants and e-moderators;
- reusable and easy to try out, recycle, reuse and change: they improve the more they are deployed and adapted.

E-tivities are valuable for:

- forming a whole course or programme when sequenced with care; also useful if you want to try out one or two online activities;
- encouraging a very wide variety of contributions and perspectives and for tapping into participants' up-to-date ideas and authentic experiences;
- replacing or supporting all other learning and teaching methods;
- any discipline, professionals or field of learning and for all topics.

The purposes of e-tivities are to:

- enable academics, designers, curriculum developers and teachers to design for online participation by their students;
- provide learners with an effective scaffold to support them in achieving the learning outcomes;
- enable learners and e-moderators to work together on key learning resources;
- promote a learner-centred, task or problem-based approach to online learning (moving away from content-centric design);
- challenge and motivate participants to critique, contribute, review and consolidate ideas in a focused way;
- increase learner engagement;
- save staff time;
- make the course productive and fun;
- easily deploy the newer technologies such as social media;
- easily find purposeful ways of using freely available, topical and/or fun resources within the learning design;
- quickly incorporate sound pedagogical principles into teaching and learning, including into large-scale online approaches such as MOOCs (massive open online courses).

To design e-tivities, you need to:

- have a way of thinking about the purpose and process of each e-tivity, and get it into draft format (the storyboard);
- work out how to place it ultimately into a learning sequence (the scaffold);
- write it in such a way that it can be placed online and participants can follow it (the invitation).

Who's who in e-tivities

Participants

I refer to all online learners, students and contributors taking part in e-tivities by the term 'participants'.

E-tivities designers

Designers create the future! The person who understands the purpose of the online encounters through the learning outcomes and objectives needs to be involved in designing. This person might be the learning designer, academic or teacher who is setting up the online experience and who ultimately may also be the e-moderator. Sometimes there are two or three people and others working together—e-tivities get designed well with three!

Students can also help with design. When they become experienced, they too can become e-tivity designers.

Or, if large numbers of online participants are involved, the person or small team doing the designing of the e-tivities may be different from the person or persons delivering the course. Sometimes one small team can design and prepare e-tivities and then many e-moderators may be needed to deliver them.

Small multiple professional teams can work together on e-tivities—we call this process 'Carpe Diem' (see Chapter 5, page 73 and Resources for Practitioners, page 186).

E-moderators

I call the trainers, instructors, facilitators or teachers 'e-moderators' because they intervene and support the e-learning. The name describes the different role that each adopts online when compared to teaching face-to-face. There is much more about e-moderators in my 2011 book, *E-moderating*.

The role of the e-moderator is the promoter and mediator of the learning through e-tivities, rather than a content expert. The e-moderator needs to know enough about the topic to weave (adding value by pulling contributions together), summarize (closing off a topic, giving teaching points), give feedback and support and enable development, pacing and challenge to happen.

Stories from the front line I

Swinburne Online (swinburneonline.com.au) in Australia provides university programmes based on e-tivities and the five-stage model (see Chapter 2), creating an immersive online experience for participants. Chapter 5 describes more ways of designing e-tivities through collaborative teams, which form the basis of Swinburne Online's design work.

Professor Kay Lipson, Academic Dean for Swinburne Online, tells us more:

In order to ensure that students are exposed to a consistent, pedagogically sound online learning experience, Swinburne Online has successfully developed an explicit set of principles that guide both learning design and delivery.

The learning design process is a collaboration between academics who are the university's discipline specialists and a learning design team with expertise in online pedagogy, educational technology, online resource acquisition and copyright. Together they design and develop an online learning experience for students that is scaffolded by e-tivities. Each e-tivity is carefully created to ensure that students are engaging meaningfully with their learning materials, their learning advisors and each other.

Learning delivery is conceptualized as a learning journey undertaken by the students and their learning advisors, taking a path navigated by e-tivities. The learning advisors take the role of e-moderators. They facilitate, question and encourage their participant groups. They aim to develop in each student and group an understanding of the relevant knowledge domain as well as a capacity for reflection and self-evaluation. Many of the learning advisors are not traditional academics, but experienced practitioners in their field, trained for their e-moderating roles.

Technology for e-tivities

E-mail, chat groups, bulletin boards and computer-mediated conferencing were developed to enable interaction between people. If a voice or text message is sent, the writer expects a response from some other person. This key characteristic can be harnessed for the purpose of interaction and engagement.

Some of the tools and platforms that we deploy are multipurpose, such as learning management systems (LMSs) and virtual learning environments

(VLEs). Throughout this book I refer to them interchangeably as LMS/VLE. Many others were developed for social purposes or for entertainment, communication or business. More about those in Chapter 4, page 57.

I hope to show you that the technologies for e-tivities can promote engagement and activity if they are appropriately used. Promoting robust and usable knowledge through engaging learners in authentic tasks and situations is critically important (Herrington, Reeves and Oliver, 2010).

Combining new ideas about mediation for learning and teaching through technologies and well-established learning theories results in fantastic poss-ibilities, but they need a little human time and energy to get them to work. High-quality interaction, full participation and reflection do not happen simply by providing the technology; hence the need to design e-tivities carefully, to reduce barriers and to enhance the technology's potential.

Many teachers and trainers at all levels of education are influenced strongly by how they themselves were taught. Most have not grown up learning to take an active part in remote or scattered groups, nor those spanning many different time zones. Many educators miss opportunities for working com-fortably and effectively online because they assume that online co-operation and collaboration need to follow similar patterns to classroom interaction (Ehrmann, 2012). The patterns and processes of e-tivities are different, although they draw on the best traditions of active group learning.

Some students are concerned about learning online, even those who are familiar with social media. They see reduced social contact in learning contexts as a real threat. They are anxious about the lack of stimulus and fun from their 'buddies' and the potential loss of a special relationship with their teachers, trainers and professors. Somehow, without them, they believe a little magic seems lost! Hence learners need support to develop the skills of working together through interactive technologies of all kinds as well as online contact with leaders and teachers. E-tivities are an answer because they focus on contributing and achieving together.

Creating the future through learning design

E-tivities are best designed and produced in advance of the participants arriving online. Good design processes result in more explicit and higher-quality activity by the participants and enable the development of more effective learning environments and interventions (Conole, 2012). By becoming an e-tivity designer, you are building in a *quality* learning experience.

E-tivities acknowledge teaching 'as a design science' based on continuous collaborative improvement and adaption in practice (Laurillard, 2012, pp. 8–9) and are a way of accessing and digitally applying teachers' creativity, vision and inspiration (Scharmer, 2009). E-tivities are very firmly rooted in learner-centred and technology-enhanced design in an increasing complex, rapidly changing digital world (Sharpe, Beetham and De Freitas, 2010). E-tivities are a way of actually taking part in the 'game changing' that is gathering pace across all types of educational provision (Oblinger, 2012; Bonk, 2009; Ellis and Goodyear, 2010). They offer a viable, principled and practical approach. They acknowledge human systems for learning by developing and evolving; they tend towards order and organization, but via messy experimentation rather than forced imposition. Order arises out of shared values and common interests (Wenger, White and Smith, 2009).

Preparing effective online learning material is a very expensive business in terms of both actual and opportunity costs. It's brought many organizations to their knees! Few academics or teachers have all the necessary skills, the time or the desire to spend months creating texts and video. Usually there will need to be an ongoing project with one or more subject experts, instructional designers and Web developers. If innovation is required, then add mobile app developers, information specialists, video developers and more.

Some people are very interested in comparisons between working online and traditional face-to-face learning. Others want to talk about the differences between online and print-based distance learning. In practice the benefits and costs are very different compared to campus-based learning. One thing we do know is that the cost of traditional ways of producing materials for online courses is very high, but savings can be made on 'delivery' (Rumble, 2010). E-tivities help with saving costs because they use existing resources, are reusable and adaptable and are based on the participants' exchange of knowledge.

Quality assurance and evaluation processes are essential too, but they add time and require extra effort. Surprisingly, many teaching and learning organizations still start by developing resources of this kind, as they seem to be the safest 'way in' to e-learning. Then they find that there are no quick fixes, only expensive experiments and 'pilots' that fail to lead to 'scale-up'.

Rather than pursuing such developments, organizations should know that e-tivities are lower risk, lower cost and a better place to begin—they inform prototyping and decision making too. If e-tivity development is built into a structured local team process, then capability is built up across the organization (see Chapter 5).

The participants' experience of learning through e-tivities

Working with others online can be playful, liberating and releasing. Online participants are often more willing to try things out in a dynamic way than they would be face-to-face, which means that e-tivities can be more fun and still promote learning. Emotions can often surface and be expressed when they could not do so in face-to-face situations. We know that involving emotions helps to promote reflectiveness (Moon, 2006).

In the search for engagement of learners, e-tivities have proven to have a special place. New online participants wrote to me about their experiences:

> It is a very special and unique experience for me. To send a message to our online conference is like talking (writing) right out in the air—to everyone and no one!? I'm just crawling about online . . . And when I get an answer back . . . I'm amazed! KO

> Excuse me where exactly am I? Do I go through a new kind of looking glass into my lecture hall? Why do my words dance as if on a stage? MO

> Thank you for the invitation to take part. I know what I'm meant to do, and even who I am meant to do it with . . . but tell me, where are the drinks? PP

> It's fun, it's new. I like being involved. Before, the telephone was the master, now its text on the screen. My own personal access to the world! So much contact, so much at my fingertips. I feel skippy inside. It's so unexpected sometimes. It's cool. PS

Participants who are working in a language other than their own have a particularly sharp learning curve. This participant reported her experience:

> Last year I felt that before I could post anything, it had to be perfect! Then sometimes I was too late, simply because the discussion had moved on. This year, I saw native speakers make mistakes too. They mistype

words or they write as they would speak, and then I felt more self-confident! I said to myself, 'It needn't be perfect, why don't you just try and join in?' And this is what I did! Maybe sometimes it was nonsense, but at least I tried, and I think text communication can only work online if you say something and somebody else says, 'yes, but' . . . and then maybe make you think again. So it was also new to me that you can write something and it's still like speaking to somebody, and you can always correct yourself or add things. GB

Teachers as e-tivity designers

Many traditional teachers are surprised at how much learning can go on through structured online networking. You might be interested in this e-mail I had from a colleague, a very experienced distance learning teacher in the UK Open University Business School.

Stories from the front line 2

Transforming the group experience

Don led a team that produced a residential weekend school; then, with a colleague, he turned to the task of preparing an online equivalent of the residential school. He e-mailed me about his experiences.

We thought our job was to write the programme for the residential school. If we thought about the online version at all, we saw it as something that would be an imitation of the residential. We never said 'pale imitation', but I sense that the categorization was there in our minds.

How wrong we were. How much the preparation—the design, the reworking of the residential material—and the observation of the online school in action have changed my mind. The online school revealed itself as a remarkable event. As we worked on the design, and as we subsequently observed the virtual exchanges, so the remarkable features of the online environment came into view, one by one.

At residential schools, the contributions by the students are oral, short and immediate. During the sales and marketing role-play exercise, students air their initial thoughts on the task, and the only sources of ideas, concepts and models from the course are the students' own memories. One member typically captures these ideas, in abbreviated form, on a flip chart. By contrast, online, everyone has a full record of everything that has been 'said'. The contributions are considered in a way that is not possible at face-to-face schools. There is scope for thoughtfulness and for reflection.

The role of the face-to-face tutor also differs from the role of e-moderator. At the residential school, the tutor may join a group for a while, sense what's going on and contribute as judgement directs, then leave. The tutor also acts as a 'postperson'—to deliver the handouts! Because the e-moderator hears (reads) everything that is said (written) and can contribute, in an equally permanent fashion, without disturbing the discussion, the online experience challenges this familiar model. A student posts a thoughtful message, which is read not only by the group but by the e-moderator too. Another follows this. The e-moderator acts more as a commentator than a facilitator in such a circumstance. Online, not only does the e-moderator post the handout but he or she can also comment on it—act as a mediator between the content and the learning.

Don Cooper, Open University Business School

Accepting the challenge

The work from which this book is derived is very much in the action research tradition. Action research involves the exploration of many aspects of online teaching through research into practice and experience. You can read about my methods in Salmon (2002b, 2004 and 2011). I have tried as much as possible to weave the principles into practice-based advice and examples.

To be successful in designing and running e-tivities you will need some passion and commitment. Designing for online involves shifting time about and changing patterns of how you work with colleagues and students. It involves setting up a computer and getting the software to work to your satisfaction, which may include going cap-in-hand to others for help. You may need to rethink your teaching and consider what is really important about the subject matter you want to teach. I hope to shine a light on a pathway for making all this more manageable and productive. It's great fun when it works. It has its own momentum. Just try it—it'll turn you into an action researcher, collaborating with your learners. Indeed, I think it's time to harness the power of online learning for our purposes. You may think this fanciful, but read on and then try it and see. This book is full of the magic of those who have trodden the path just Internet moments before you. Just try it.

Chapter 2

E-tivities in the five-stage model

For online learning to be successful and happy, participants need to be supported through a structured developmental process. This chapter offers a description of my five-stage model, which provides a framework or scaffold for a structured and paced programme of e-tivities. A structured learning scaffold implies prior design, providing a familiar and sequenced routine leading to increasing control by the learner.

The five-stage model offers essential support and development to participants at each stage as they build up expertise in learning online. Each stage requires e-tivities of a different nature, as I will outline.

Introducing the model

First, I will briefly explain the five-stage model. There's a much fuller description, along with the research on which it is based, in the third edition of *E-moderating* (Salmon, 2011).

The model shows how participants can benefit from increasing skill and comfort in working, networking and learning online, and what the person or people providing the human support (I call them e-moderators) needs to do at each stage to help them to achieve this success. The model also shows how to motivate online participants, to build their learning through appropriate e-tivities and to pace them through programmes of education and development.

Nearly all participants will progress through the five stages, provided that they are given good instructions (invitations) on how to work together, appropriate e-tivities to promote action and interaction, motivation through both purpose and feedback—and necessary technical support. Stages 3 and 5 are the more productive and constructive stages, but they work much better for everyone if participants have taken part first in e-tivities pitched at Stages 1 and 2.

For learners at Stage 1, at the base of the flight of steps in Figure 2.1, individual access and purposeful reasons to go on frequently and repeatedly throughout the ongoing learning and community process are essential prerequisites for full participation and engagement.

Stage 2 involves individual participants establishing their online identities and then finding others with whom to interact. They start to understand the benefits and requirements of working with others in their online environments.

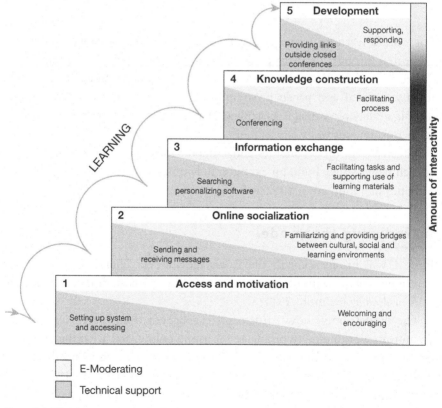

Figure 2.1 The five-stage model of teaching and learning online

At Stage 3, participants engage in mutual exchange of information and make learning-related contributions. Up to and including Stage 3, a form of co-operation occurs whereby each person supports the other participants' goals.

At Stage 4, course-related group discussions and activities develop and the interaction becomes collaborative, more team-orientated and more complex. Knowledge construction begins.

At Stage 5, participants are comfortable working together online and develop an ability to exploit fully the benefits for their learning. They are free, active and confident in further pursuing ideas and goals, discovering, reflecting and presenting for assessment.

Each stage requires participants to have the minimum capability to exploit the e-learning platform or environment in use (shown in the bottom left of each step). Each stage calls for different e-moderating skills (shown on the right top of each step).

The 'interactivity bar' running along the right of the flight of steps suggests the intensity of participation that you can expect at each stage. At first, at Stage 1, participants interact with only one or two others. After Stage 2, the numbers of others with whom they interact, and the frequency of their inter-actions gradually increases, although Stage 5 often sees a return to more individual and small group pursuits.

Participants will differ in the amount of time each will need at every stage before progressing. For example, the model applies to all online learning software, but if experienced participants are introduced to online learning platforms that are new to them, they will tend to linger for a while at Stages 1 or 2 but then move on quite rapidly through the stages. People are likely to cycle through the model many times as they increase their knowledge and explore their learning in different domains. More experienced participants will move more rapidly towards Stages 4 and 5, often helping those less experienced online. E-tivities must be designed for each stage in sequence. E-moderators can aim to ensure participants working in cohorts move on to a new stage at the same time.

A benefit of using the model to design development processes and build a programme of e-tivities for online learning is that you will know how indi-viduals are likely to exploit the system at each stage. You can pitch the e-tivities to what the majority needs at each stage and you can thus avoid common pitfalls. Your design effort will pay off: there will be active online learning, good contri-butions, interaction between participants and increased student satisfaction. E-moderators who understand the model and apply it should enjoy their work more: they are likely to spend less time trying to recruit recalcitrant participants, more time supporting creative e-tivities and giving essential feedback.

E-tivity design for the five stages

Novices solve problems by following step-by-step procedures, so early e-tivities need to include these. As participants gain competence and expertise, they can handle much more complex ideas. Hence the knowledge useful to novices is different from the knowledge useful to experienced practitioners or learners. In other words, it's our picture of our participants—their needs and competencies and the stage they are at—that determines the tone and focus of the e-tivity. Essentially, you need to be explicit about the group's development and the nature of the tasks at each stage. You can then draw on ideas of gradual group development and the scaffolding (Pea, 2004) provided by the five-stage model.

Below are some ideas to underpin the process of thinking through e-tivities at each stage of the model. See Resources for Practitioners 1 for many more examples.

Stage 1: Access and motivation

One key issue at Stage 1 is ensuring that your participants have easy access to the platforms, systems and processes in use. Not just once but many times, all the time. Another is whether your participants are being motivated to spend time and effort, and keep on returning to take part. There is a complex interplay between the participants' technical access and skills and the motivation to be active online, but the main reason why participants keep coming back is to see if anyone has responded to their messages.

E-moderators should not be complacent about participants' entry level skills to online learning. There are still many novices, even people who are very frequent social networkers. However, what really matters here is acquiring the emotional and social capacity to learn with others online. Technical skills can be acquired and changed as needs be. Participants' feelings about being unable to take part successfully are more significant than their precise technical skills.

Access

Let's consider the issue of access to the system first. At this first stage the participants need good, regular access to the online environment and link-perfect navigation. They need sufficient knowledge to find the most important parts of it on screen or their mobile device. If they are to be fully engaged in their online learning, then they need to know how to take part actively, not just how to find and read the screen content.

Figure 2.2 Stage 1: our new learner, Mo, sets off on his e-tivities journey

At Stage 1, the technical skills of participants and staff will vary enormously. Many people will be unfamiliar with the software tools you choose to use. It is important to show participants how to use the software but this needs to be achieved whilst they are taking part in online e-tivities that are interesting and relevant to them. Even participants who use the Internet daily in their social and professional lives need time and support.

New students in Swinburne Online courses reflected on their first week:

> Beginning online learning has been an experience, to say the least! I was uncomfortable using the site at the start of the week. Especially since usually all I use the Internet for is Facebook and YouTube . . . As I use the [Swinburne] Learn site, I have become more comfortable, although I am by no means confident yet. DP

E-tivities at this stage therefore need to provide a gentle but interesting introduction to using the technological platform and opportunities for acknowledgement of the feelings surrounding using technology. The key is to enable participants to feel that help is at hand and to ensure that e-tivities foster an environment in which participants feel at ease and not alone as they tackle their digital frontier:

> After some dramas in enrolment, Friday afternoon of Week 1, I rang the helpdesk . . . Put through to the helpful guys in IT who, thankfully, didn't finish at 5pm! So glad to read through all your posts in the e-tivities and feel I was with real-life, like-minded people. So far, between phone contact, IT help, and posts from fellow students and our e-learning advisor, I feel I am part of a supportive environment. That is always a good place to be. Thank you to all who contribute to this and I hope I can be equally supportive as we go through the study. RD

Motivation

At Stage 1, first focus on building e-tivities that enable participants to become involved, contribute and develop skills. Stage 1 e-tivities should directly enable participants to increase their comfort with the use of the technology in an integrated and worthwhile way for them. You may have greater success through a stealth method than attempting to directly teach online learning skills or the use of a particular platform.

The key is to mobilize participants' understanding about why they are learning, why in this way, as well as what they have to do to take part. Motivators should be integrally involved in your e-tivities as part of both the process and the experience. Motivation is not something that you can set out to 'apply' or create on its own.

As an aside, it's clear that negatives along the lines of 'bad dog—no biscuit' are not successful! Nor is it useful to assume that awarding marks for contribution will be a motivator. Furthermore, it is just so easy to demotivate e-learners at this stage, as many may believe that they have to get over the hurdle of becoming familiar with the technology, of 'meeting' with classmates and exposing their own ignorance. An uninteresting e-tivity or a chance unfortunate remark can be a strong demotivator.

There are many different ways to promote motivation. You will need to decide clearly how many you can incorporate into your e-tivities at this early stage! One way to consider motivation at Stage 1 is in terms of expectancy theory (Biggs and Tang, 2011). Expectancy theory says that the learning activity must have value to the learner and that the learner must expect to succeed. So clarity of purpose from e-tivity designers and e-moderators is critical from the very beginning. To demonstrate value at Stage 1, make it very clear to participants the purpose of your programmes of e-tivities (for them) or how Stage 1 links to and integrates with the rest of the learning or networking process, its role in assessed components (tests and assignments) and the amount of time they should allocate to working on it. It is important to clarify the purpose of each e-tivity at the beginning of each invitational message.

It is a great mistake to assume that any participant will want to dedicate hours and hours to online learning without good reason, or will be motivated by a good range of readings and videos alone.

Demonstrating how to succeed is harder than it sounds. In different learning and teaching cultures, disciplines and educational levels, the meaning of success may vary. So, when designing an e-tivity, it is important to specify the purpose clearly and make it achievable. At Stage 1, even simple e-tivities may need a considerable amount of time and support to work well.

Some people respond best to 'achievement' motivation. They need tasks that they can reasonably easily achieve—ones that are neither too hard nor too easy (McClelland, 1985). Others will need 'competence' motivation. This refers to participants' belief in their ability to achieve, what (to them) may seem a difficult task. At Stage 1, e-tivities need to be easier than at Stage 2, Stage 2 e-tivities less challenging than Stage 3, and so on. This means that the more difficult and demanding e-tivities should be introduced from Stages 3 and 4 onwards, and even then gradually.

Expectancy theory suggests two main kinds of motivation: 'extrinsic' and 'intrinsic'. Extrinsic motivation includes positive reinforcement and rewards (e.g. a financial incentive or marks) or negative reinforcement (such as punishment). In extrinsic motivation the student focuses on the outcome. With increasing importance being placed on outcomes in learning, the clarity of extrinsic motivators is critically important.

A second kind of expectancy-based motivation is intrinsic. Here the participants learn because they are happy to take part in the activity for its own sake. The more you are able to build group and team feelings, the more effective intrinsic motivation will be. It also lasts longer.

It is unlikely that participants other than very experienced e-learners will exhibit high levels of intrinsic motivation at Stage 1. However, you will observe intrinsic motivators operating successfully at Stages 3 to 5.

Another potential motivator is 'social'. Essentially, participants 'learn to please people whose opinions are important to them' (Biggs and Tang, 2011, p. 35). Typical examples may be parents, the boss or the e-moderator. This kind of focusing can lead to participants 'picking out' messages of those people who are important to them online, especially if there are many messages. Concentrate on making group work important.

So to summarize: e-tivities at Stage 1 should concentrate on providing motivation and set the pace and rhythm for the rest of the course. Participants need to gain experience in the technology in use without believing it to be what the course is about. Therefore e-tivities need to be designed carefully to enable the participants to find their way around the online learning platform whilst taking part in relevant and authentic tasks that involve others. E-tivities need to be motivating throughout—however, they can become more intrinsic from Stage 2 onwards.

There may be some anxiety at this stage about how participants are expected to behave and who is online with them. This will not be visible to the e-moderator unless expressed in messages. Make a start on e-tivities that address these concerns and help people to feel more comfortable. Try to avoid the 'say who you are', 'post a photo' and 'fill in your profile' type of message. At the start of a unit or programme, such messages frighten some people, particularly the more reticent or less experienced in the online environment, and are typically unfocused and unproductive to summarize.

If you would like a summary of advice on motivation have a look at Resources for Practitioners 13, pages 168–9.

Arriving

Allow plenty of time for this stage. Participants simply will not all log in on the day and at the time that you plan. A few will come a little early and may race ahead. Some will come late. Allow at least a week for everyone to log on, get started and complete the first few e-tivities. You will know this stage is over when the majority of your expected participants are online and the rest are giving 'life got in the way', rather than 'the technology doesn't work' type of excuses. Four or five short e-tivities can be completed within week 1 addressing Stage 1 and it's fine to plan accordingly. Make it very clear to participants that you expect everyone to have completed these introductory e-tivities by the end of week 1 and that all need to move on together to week 2.

In addition, those who are online will be showing some proficiency, at least in finding where to interact, and in posting messages that go beyond 'Help, where am I?' and 'Why am I here?'.

Stage 2: Online socialization

At Stage 2, you are doing nothing less than creating your own micro-community through active and interactive e-tivities. Whether the community will last a few weeks or a few years, it is a very special learning and teaching opportunity.

E-tivities at Stage 2 need to focus on enabling participants to relate to a few others and on reasonably stretching tasks. E-tivities at this stage should provide ways of knowing who else is in the shared space and how this knowledge can be used to guide participants' work.

Provide practice, practice and practice—not in the technology, but in working together!

At Stage 2 we need to promote webs of trust that do not depend on physically meeting. Online, people have the ability to convey feelings and build relationships. This is not a demanding concept to understand, but in the rush to 'get on with the learning' it is frequently missed. Online teams or small communities must be built up for engagement between participants to occur, and relevant authentic and purposeful e-learning activities must also be simultaneously introduced to sustain the community.

I need to make myself clear here: the *lack* of face-to-face and visual clues in online participation is a key ingredient of equity and success rather than a

Figure 2.3 Stage 2: Mo learns how to contribute to the learning of the group
through e-tivities

barrier. If the remoteness and virtuality are handled appropriately, they can increase the comfort level of e-moderators and participants alike. Therefore I do not consider that (interactive) e-learning is deficient for teaching and learning. Instead it brings its own special advantages and disadvantages compared to face-to-face working (Friesen, 2011). Participants report that online socialization is integral to their learning depth, sense of cohesion and emotional support (Holley and Taylor, 2009). So we have an excellent opportunity here to establish amazing and real opportunities for cross-cultural, cross-disciplinary learning.

So, to work together really productively at the later stages, participants need not only to get to know each other's online personae and approaches but also to understand each other's hopes, aspirations, goals and dreams. All right, maybe not the dreams at this stage. Be prepared to be amazed at how well supportive and productive links between people are created if you create the right opportunities. The role of carefully chosen e-tivities at Stage 2 is to build bridges between the intentions and the achievements.

When designing effective e-tivities for Stage 2, consider what it feels like and means to enter a new and fresh world with people from a wide variety of backgrounds and perhaps cultures and countries. When asynchronous computer-based learning first started, there was a belief that there would be a strong discontinuity between people's location-based physical selves and their online or virtual personae. We now know that this is not the case—and that online learning groups can and do develop their own strong identities.

I find the ideas of a community of practice are helpful in this context. Wenger (2006) tells us that there are three main components of a community of practice: joint enterprise, mutuality and shared repertoire.

Joint enterprise means that, at Stage 2, you need to help your participants understand the value of learning together online and enable them to get to know how they might do this—in particular, how they might each contribute to group work. Mutuality means that they gradually come to trust each other. Writing online often involves in-depth sharing of ideas and support: you design e-tivities to encourage exploration though writing. Developing a shared repertoire includes exploring 'language, routines, sensibilities, artefacts, tools, stories, styles' (Wenger, 2000, p. 229; see also Wenger et al., 2009). E-tivities at this stage thus need to directly offer opportunities to share and develop a repertoire for the group. No technology, however sophisticated, will create such a culture. At best the technology will enable it to grow, once established. Sensitive and appropriate e-tivities and the e-moderator's interventions create the conditions for effective online socialization.

Stage 2 e-tivities should offer experience in developing sensitivity to gender, racial issues, potential personality conflicts and various educational values and expectations. Relate e-tivities at Stage 2 to the traditions of your topic, discipline, profession or organization—thus providing the important cultural contexts for learning and making later knowledge construction easier to achieve. To promote groups and achieve much more collaborative learning later on, e-tivities about exploring cultural knowledge are very valuable at this stage, particularly those that explain differences. By culture, here I mean differences in disciplines of learning or professions as well as countries.

Bear in mind that participants will almost certainly be involved in a variety of social networking communities and also learning and practice at the same time. Some of these may be similar in values, beliefs and norms of behaviour to those of your own groups and some may not. Therefore the design should be purposeful and focused to ensure that a compatible and achieving community is built. This is truly a process of socialization, and can leave out those on the margins of understanding unless e-tivities explicitly ensure inclusion (Lauzon, 2000).

One of the most important lessons about cross-cultural interaction is that tolerance and effectiveness emerge from greater understanding of multiple perspectives and points of view (Osland, Bird and Mendenall, 2012). So e-tivities at this stage need to concentrate on surfacing and exploring viewpoints. After views and plans are offered, the group can examine them. Where differences are small, agreement can be assumed but there can be little learning unless differences are surfaced and discussed. New understandings arise from exploring different perspectives—although a shared framework is necessary for this to occur (Tolmie and Boyle, 2000). If differences are too great, the e-tivity is unlikely to get off the ground. What you're aiming to achieve here is to expose differences enough to result in the creation of new understandings, but within a shared framework of activity so that participants are neither under-stimulated nor overwhelmed at any one time.

Both participants and e-moderators should be aware at this stage that their characterizations of other cultures are 'best guesses' (Bird and Osland, 2005). Exploring cultural differences and alternative understandings at this stage is usually undertaken with good humour, though sometimes people can be upset. What you are looking for here is recognition that each individual or group has something unique and special to offer (Goodfellow and Lamy, 2009). Later, at Stage 4, more of a 'peeling away' of layers can be encouraged.

Stage 2 is over when participants start to share something of themselves online, show some competency and less anxiety about the nature of the platform in use and are interested and engaged around your topics and e-tivities. Many e-tivities designers are keen to rush on from this stage but it is the foundation for future engaged online learning and needs considerable investment from everyone. It's worth it—you will have the participants with you and effectively working together, and at greater depth, very soon. The basis for future information exchange and knowledge construction will have been laid down.

Essentially, you are looking for the majority of members to have some understanding about the group or community's ability to work together online and how they might contribute to their own and others' learning and development through this medium. They should be interacting with each other, and between them some trust should be starting to build up. They should be sharing stories and ideas, and exploring styles and ways of working.

Designers or e-moderators should ensure that the social side of interactive media continues to be available for those who want it. Either ask students to set up their own processes or have a social media group prepared for them.

Stage 3: Information exchange

At Stage 3, information can be exchanged and co-operative tasks can be achieved. The big advantage of using an asynchronous environment is that everyone can explore information at their own pace and react to it before hearing the views and interpretations of others. E-tivities allow for this key component of group learning.

Participants' learning requires two kinds of interaction: interaction with the course materials, with a strong focus on learning outcomes and objectives, and interaction with people, namely the e-moderator(s) and other participants.

See Resources for Practitioners 21, pages 191–3 for examples of how to 'storyboard' and to integrate topics and participation.

E-tivities at Stage 3 should have a very strong task and action focus. Use them to enable participants to impart information to each other and to explain, explore and clarify. They should be shown how to provide feedback to each other in the spirit of deepening understanding. This will help them in preparing to move on to Stage 4 e-tivities.

At Stage 3, I suggest that you also have a strong notion of scaffolding, of helping participants to both deepen their understanding and their ability to work constructively with each other. Design for them e-tivities that focus on exploring co-ordination and communication between the participants so that each works towards his or her own objectives. Do not demand or expect massive collaboration just yet.

Figure 2.4 Stage 3: Mo engages with the learning

At this stage, you can experiment with the structure of groups and the techniques for group working. You will still need to be clear about which groups are assigned which parts of each task. You could also try buzz groups (each group is given a topic) or syndicates (each group has an assigned task), which culminate in a plenary debate (Jaques and Salmon, 2008).

Participants need to know about tools for remote access to information and about strategies for purposeful information retrieval, but the information in the e-tivities invitation should be brief to initiate action and interaction. Even at Stage 3, if participants have to find and read masses of information online this will divert them from active and interactive learning.

At this stage, participants may look to the e-moderators to provide direction, through the mass of messages and encouragement, to start using the most relevant material. E-moderators should provide regular weaving, feedback, summaries and plenaries. One of the commonest questions teachers ask me is 'How do I keep them motivated?'.

This is how. When participants start using e-tivities, the twists of time and complexity can elicit quite uncomfortable, confused reactions from some participants and anxiety in a few. This may be because they were expecting to sit back to a lecture. Structure, pacing and clear expectations of participants should be provided, both for the scaffolding process as a whole and for each e-tivity. Clear prior instructions on timing and occasional weaving by the e-moderator will help to sustain motivation and establish presence.

At Stage 3, the learning designer should ensure that e-tivities concentrate on discovering or exploring aspects of information known to participants, or reasonably easily retrieved by them. E-tivities that encourage the presenting and linking of data, analysis and ideas in interesting ways online will stimulate productive information sharing.

Stage 3 is over when participants have learned how to find, contribute and exchange information productively and successfully through e-tivities, and when the number of people lurking, browsing or 'vicariously learning' are minimal. When you notice that your participants are challenging the basis of an e-tivity, or want to change it, or suggest alternatives to the spark that you have provided, then you will know that they are ready for Stage 4. Participants must acquire familiarity with the technology by Stage 3—if they have not, then it will prove a distraction from the much more demanding e-tivities and relationships that develop at Stage 4. Participants should also understand both the general dynamics of group working and how their particular group can operate successfully. I think by now you will have spotted that these online skills are gradually learned through scaffolding the e-tivities, not by demands, posting the theories and running separate 'training' sessions.

Stage 4: Knowledge construction

By Stage 4, many participants begin to recognize the great potential of online interaction and they start to take control of their own knowledge construction.

Thinking is the key to making information useful (McDermott, 1999). From this stage onwards, you can develop e-tivities that promote the processes of thinking and interacting with others online. Sternberg (2010) suggests that these skills include:

- critical, analytical thinking including judging, evaluating, comparing and contrasting and assessing;
- creative thinking including discovering, inventing, imagining and hypothesizing;
- practical thinking including applying, using and practising.

Learners build their own internal representations of knowledge, linking it directly to personal experience. This personal knowledge is constantly open to change. Each piece of newly constructed knowledge is actively built on previous knowledge (Lauzon, 2000). Where we seek to engender practical knowledge, we need to draw on e-tivities that enable participants not just to 'cut and paste' best practice from the past to the current situation but also to draw from their own experience. At Stage 4, we see participants start to become online authors, rather than receivers or transmitters of information. The development of tacit knowledge and its potential impact on practice can emerge strongly at this stage.

E-tivities at Stage 4 can draw on these opportunities. E-tivities at this stage have knowledge development at their core. Sparks are still important but ultimately the participants need to structure knowledge for themselves. The challenge in designing the e-tivities is to strike a balance between providing too much structure and too little. What is important is what the participants make of the e-tivities. E-tivities can be based on sparks or questions that have no obvious right or wrong answers. The e-tivities can offer knowledge building (rather than exchange of information) or a series of ideas or challenges, but avoid putting multiple questions in one e-tivity. Providing sequenced small e-tivities works better. It's the designer's responsibility to sequence them! The topics are likely to be strategic, problem- or practice-based ones. E-tivities that encourage exploration and interpretation of wider issues will hone the skills of operating cross-culturally across disciplines and professions. E-tivities can introduce the idea that there may be multiple perspectives and solutions.

Figure 2.5 Stage 4: Mo constructs knowledge with his group

Objectives at Stage 4 can be related to broadening understanding, providing different viewpoints, perspectives and examples. Avoid specifying in advance exactly what has to be learned at this point, but ground your e-tivities in real-world contexts and define the processes for producing the required end results.

At Stage 4, you can move increasingly towards peer-directed e-tivities and participant work teams. For example, you could try defining a group outcome, or asking the group to provide its own goal and objectives, then give directions on how to collaborate.

Discussion-based e-tivities can work well and can be used so long as they are structured and focused. Develop e-tivities that have a wide variety of interpretations and perspectives (multiple realities), because this will encourage dialogue and collaboration, including constructive critique, debate and disagreement. E-tivities can include choosing from alternatives, choosing thoughtfully (and giving reasons and arguments for choices), affirming a choice and giving proposals for improving practice and skills, and acting upon choices.

You can increase the information that you offer as a 'spark', if you wish, after your students have become adept at working online, at managing their time and at working with each other—in other words, when they have arrived at Stage 4.

The best e-tivities at this stage aim at building and constructing appropriate knowledge created from the previous e-tivities. Within this activity participants may draw on previous knowledge acquisition and collaborative learning, including the e-moderators' weaves and summaries, and apply this to dilemmas or problem solving. These tasks enable participants to reflect critically on their previous learning, on their own understanding of it, and to apply it practically and appropriately. In their responses participants are required to define their own understanding, as well as to critique, enhance and collaborate with others about their understanding, thus constructing and demonstrating their knowledge in more than one dimension.

Stage 4 can be considered completed when a joint outcome has been produced or there is an independent collaborative e-tivity in evidence. Once you've got participants to this stage, they will have their own sense of time, place and momentum. Another clue is that they can comfortably and supportively challenge and build on each other's contributions. By then they may be able to move up and down the stages with some ease.

Stage 5: Development

At Stage 5, participants can become responsible for their own learning and that of their group. They will start to build on the ideas acquired through all

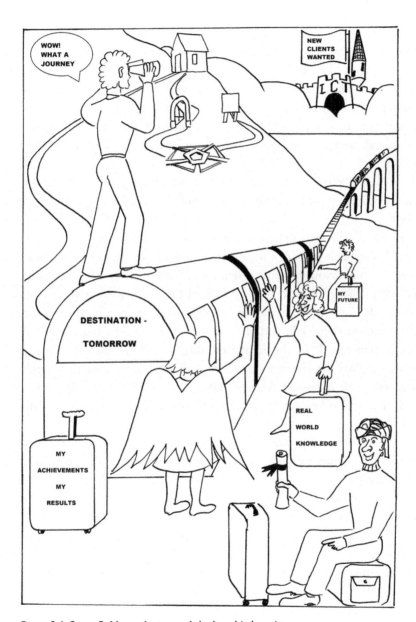

Figure 2.6 Stage 5: Mo evaluates and deploys his learning

four earlier stages of the e-tivities, and will apply them to their individual contexts. By now, participants will have stopped wondering how they can use online participation and instead become committed and creative. This will stand them in excellent stead throughout the rest of their digital lives and enable them to be contributors as well as consumers of online knowledge.

Frequently, they also become critical and truly self-reflective. Participants find ways of producing and dealing with humour and the more emotional aspects of writing and interacting. Experienced participants often become most helpful as guides to newcomers to online interaction and the technologies. Such experience and skills will help them throughout the rest of their online learning careers.

At Stage 5, the purposes behind e-tivities centre on participants gaining self-insight, reflecting and making judgements about their experience and knowledge.

Metacognitive skills refer to people's understanding and control of their own thinking. It's a valuable form of self-awareness and impacts on a learner's ability to self-regulate behaviours (Gunawardena et al., 2009). If you have engaged your participants carefully and fully at each of the previous four stages, you will be rewarded by explicit evidence of their metacognition by Stage 5 and be able to promote their skills and offer very challenging e-tivities. Stick with the familiar framework of the invitation though. Metacognitive learning skills focus on what the learners do in new contexts or on how they might apply concepts and ideas (de Andres Martinez, 2012). These skills can be fostered at Stage 5, and e-tivities to address them, such as development plans, are valuable.

Develop e-tivities that enable evaluation and critiquing. Ask participants to demonstrate their ability to work with arguments and examples and to defend their own judgements. Encourage them to explore their metacognitive awareness of positions they adopt—for example, 'How did you arrive at that position?' or 'Which is better and why?'. Don't forget to explore feelings and emotions about learning, as well as their experience of the topics under discussion.

Using an e-portfolio alongside e-tivities and scaffolding is very helpful to support reflecting and metacognitive skills. There is a range of educational benefits from e-portfolios (Stefani, Mason and Pegler, 2007).

There is also a crucial role for e-tivities at Stage 5 in promoting and enhancing reflection and maximizing the value of online learning for each participant (Williams et al., 2001) and for the group learning experience (Salmon, 2002a).

Moon offers a useful definition of the links between reflection and learning:

> Reflection is a form of mental processing—like a form of thinking—that we use to fulfil a purpose or to achieve some anticipated outcome. It is applied to relatively complicated or unstructured ideas for which there is not an obvious solution and is largely based on the further processing of knowledge and understanding and possibly emotions that we already possess.
>
> (Moon, 2006, p. 37)

Reflective practice offers the opportunity for individuals to engage in metacognitive strategies that enhance self-regulation and monitoring of their own learning journeys (Boulton and Hramiak, 2012).

A powerful concept and process for use in designing e-tivities is to ask participants to recall a familiar experience as a preparation for introducing them to a new one. The idea is that in attempting to understand a problem or explore a scenario, experiences need to be interrogated and perhaps tested and challenged to avoid or at least bring to light the unconscious assumptions that may reduce creativity and flexibility. A key aspect of learning through reflective processes is that each learner will have different ways of dealing with ideas—a key form of personalizing learning.

The results of participants' work on e-tivities are available for revisiting and reconsidering in a way that cannot happen with more transient verbal conversation, or classroom-based tutorials. E-tivities provide opportunities for ongoing reflective analysis, particularly when the need to reflect is built into learning tasks or assessed assignments. It is possible to 'rewind' a conversation, to pick out threads and make and build on links between different messages. Emotions can often be noticed, surfaced and expressed, and may be passed over in face-to-face situations.

Do indicate why you expect your participants to reflect. At key times during the interaction, I suggest that you pose a well-placed reflective question. Regularly ask participants to look back through the online scaffolded experience. Suggest that they revisit their own and other people's responses frequently as their learning progresses.

Desirable e-tivities at Stage 5 focus on development and further learning as the outcome of and building upon all of the previous stages. Here participants critically reflect on their learning and apply it to their own personal construction of the topic.

Chapter 3

Creating e-tivities

This chapter will help you to develop techniques for creating high-quality e-tivities for use within your course, programme, community or in any other online context. It explains how to establish enjoyable and successful e-tivities. Resources for Practitioners in Part II offers you further ideas.

The whole e-tivity process should be geared towards engaging participants in active online learning that results in achieving the outcomes that they and you desire. Therein lies the benefit for the participants and the purpose of all the pedagogical activity. This seems obvious, yet I know it is easy to become focused on providing wonderful resources or to become excited about the potential of the technology and then to wonder why people do not want to take part, or, if they do, why they experience difficulties.

That's why I call the e-tivity instructional message the 'invitation'—this word helps to remind me that I'm looking for a response from others and I'm planning a social learning event. Now's the time to take a look at what you are aiming to produce—see Tables 1.1 and 1.2, pages 2 and 3. It's on the Web in a pretty format if you'd like to download that page (www.e-tivities.com).

As an ideal, aim for participants to contribute positively, actively, constructively and interactively. I know this is easier said than done. However, I hope you will use the principles in this chapter and try out some e-tivities that seem meaningful to you. A great advantage is that they can be easily changed for a second try, or scaled up for increased numbers. Give attention to active engagement, participation, the emotional aspects of learning and new constructs of time. I know that the outcomes will surpass your best expectations!

E-tivities require careful construction. Most of the groundwork should be prepared in advance of the participants' arrival. Finding, structuring and delivering online 'content' is less important than teaching techniques when designing and running e-tivities. With good design and preparation, the e-moderator's role in running the e-tivities becomes easier and much less intense.

So let's get started!

A reminder: The overall e-tivity design process

First ask yourself (several times if necessary), or have someone else ask you or your team, the following questions. Record the answers:

- What learning outcome or objective do you want to achieve? and/or
- What pedagogical challenge or problem do you want to solve? and/or
- What key piece of knowledge do you want your learners to explore that will provide a doorway to more learning together?
- How will this activity fit—what stage of the model?

Then to design e-tivities you need to:

- Draft your first ideas—start with the end (learning outcome or objective) in mind.
- Draft a learning sequence—consider the schedule and what point of the five-stage model (the scaffold) your learners will be at.
- Write the e-tivity in a way that it can be placed online and participants can easily follow it (use the invitational framework).

Remind yourself next of some key principles:

- Write the invitation so that your participants are clear about your intended objectives for an e-tivity.
- Ensure that your planned evaluation or assessment meets the purpose(s) of the e-tivity. If assessment is involved, look for alignment with tasks. Attempts to force participation in e-tivities through direct assessment of contribution are rarely successful.
- Build in motivation as part of the process of undertaking the e-tivity itself and not as something separate from it. Motivation occurs because of the learning activities. Avoid trying to motivate people simply to log

on and 'discuss'. Instead, provide an e-tivity that makes taking part worthwhile.
- Decide what you expect the participants to do and what the e-moderators will do.
- Create an experience that is complete and worthwhile. This includes setting short-term goals but ensuring that there is a satisfying process and flow of actions. When delivering and supporting the e-tivity, the e-moderators will need to exercise judgement about when to go with the flow, when to weave and when to guide participants more explicitly towards expected outcomes.
- Be highly sensitive to timing and pacing. Divide the e-tivity up into bite-sized chunks of no more than one, two or three weeks' work for a complete e-tivity.
- If you offer more than one e-tivity at a time, build them together in a coherent way to create a sequence. Use the five-stage model.
- Ensure that the e-tivities are in some way focused on sharing, shaping, elaborating or deepening understanding. Ensure that participants need to work together in some way to achieve the learning outcomes. If you cannot see how to make working together add value to the learning, maybe using an e-tivity is not the best approach.
- Aim to provide just one invitational message per e-tivity, one that contains everything needed to take part. If the message gets complicated, divide the e-tivity into smaller e-tivities, and sequence them.

Think about the purpose of the e-tivity

I think of objectives as the stated anticipated result or outcomes of an e-tivity—what I expect it to deliver. There's great value in driving an e-tivity from a 'problem' or challenge. See, for example, Savin-Baden and Wilkie (2006). Learning outcomes mean to me what the participants can expect to get out of the experience for themselves. For e-tivities, in the spirit of constructivism, I prefer to group these objectives together and call them 'purpose'. In other words, purpose implies a somewhat broader framework or intention. By the way, with good e-tivities the outcomes are often more variable, or better, or deeper than originally intended. However, make sure that you can provide a rationale for the e-tivity in terms of purpose for your participants. Indicating the purpose of taking part to the participants is a key part of motivation. Don't feel you must define the purpose to the absolute . . . let them surprise you!

You will find that participants often want to discuss the purpose of an e-tivity among themselves. This is a productive discussion and will stimulate people to take part. The shared purpose promotes the e-tivity and gives it meaning. To keep the pace up, e-moderators may need to encourage people to 'go with the flow' and reflect later. Understandably, individual participants may have their own agendas in addition to the shared purpose.

At Stages 1, 2 and 3, you will need to state the purpose clearly at the beginning of the e-tivity. At Stages 4 and 5, purposes can be more negotiable or variations negotiated. This is how participants start to gain ownership of the learning. However, most importantly, shared understanding is needed of the task with which the participants are engaged. This is why careful pacing and consistent, clear instructions are critical.

Consider formative and summative assessment and feedback

Biggs and Tang (2011) offer us the idea of 'alignment' in teaching and assessment. Overtly separate assessment activities break the flow of the e-tivity processes. Your assessment strategies are likely to be more successful, discriminating and fair if they arise 'naturally' out of the e-tivities. There are two main ways of coming closer to compatibility between e-tivities and assessment. One is by using electronic means through the technology platform itself, and the other is by using reflective and collaborative outcomes to align assessment with the teaching and learning characteristics of e-tivities.

When developing e-tivities, we need to look right from the start at how the learning can be appropriately assessed, whether based on individual or group work. E-tivities rarely produce one 'right' answer; therefore assessment outcomes can be judged in a number of ways. Make this clear to participants.

There may be complex power and emotional issues at play, and designers and e-moderators need to be both sensitive and maintain appropriate authority (Reilly, Gallagher-Lepak and Killion, 2012). There's more in Chapter 2 of *E-moderating* about this (Salmon, 2011). However, if you succeed in getting groups of participants working productively together at Stages 4 and 5, then they are already involved in mutual and supportive feedback and in evaluation of each other's work through their ongoing interaction (Crosta and McConnell, 2008; McConnell, 2006). The scene is thus set for compatible assessment procedures. If the purpose of an e-tivity is carefully worked out, this will often give you a clue as to how it can be assessed. Or, if you're brave, you can encourage groups to design their own assessments. So essentially I'm suggesting that the principles for e-tivities also apply to assessment.

Stories from the front line 3

Sue Kokonis, Director of Teaching for the entirely digital university Swinburne Online, reports:

If the design of an e-tivity results in students recognising it as interesting, easy to understand and relevant to subsequent assessments, there is greater engagement. For the pragmatic, time-poor student they need to be convinced that doing the e-tivity adds value to their learning! Good design of e-tivities is crucial and our learning designers work with the university academics to create relevant e-tivities, tasks and actions and make the links to assessment explicit. When we get this right, students really appreciate the value of learning collaboratively. One participant commented:

> At the start of this unit I would have argued that I am the captain of my ship and my ship is only big enough for one. I need to say that, now, the opposite cannot be more true! I relish the e-tivities each week to read about other students' learning journeys. It is inspiring to me to be able to benchmark every week, but also to learn from the students. Learning online is not just about learning from the content provided; each student contributes to the learning process. We are all each other's teaching tools. As I read the thoughts from other students, it challenges my thinking. Did I really grasp the concept? This is a brilliant way to learn—I keep thinking about the content during the week and the information sticks. The learning experience is so much bigger than the teacher and I, it is the whole classroom learning together, and we really are in it together! DH

If you are evaluating or assessing outcomes of e-tivities, then you will need to indicate the level or degree of acceptable performance and how marks and grades will be allocated. Inevitably, what you will look for in assessment is the outcome that you hoped for, as well as any valid outcomes that you didn't plan for. If you don't get the outcomes you were looking for, then change something about the e-tivity for a second try next time.

The Internet has led to new methods of cheating for those learners who are inclined to do so. For example, where assessment is based on individual written work, such as essays or dissertations, use of technology may simply make it easier for participants to present work that they have not personally authored. But technology can also be used to detect cheating. (Take a look, for example, at www. plagiarism.org.) It is important to establish and publish what you mean by the difference between collaborating and cheating. All universities have policies about plagiarism and cheating that need to be reinforced in the online environment. A useful set of resources can be found on the Joint Information Systems Committee (JISC, 2012) website.

In your e-tivities, encourage participants to use, but carefully attribute, remarks and quotes from messages. There is a fine dividing line between 'compiling' or 'summarizing' and 'plagiarizing'. Perhaps you could try an e-tivity at Stage 1 or 2 to address and explore these words directly.

Successfully taking students through a scaffolded approach to learning online offers a sense of involvement and hence potentially less desire to gain an unfair advantage over other participants. Focusing on participation and contribution reduces the opportunities for plagiarism.

Consider, too, offering rewards for group working. Not only may assessment be linked to the group's individual learning outcome, but both intrinsic and extrinsic rewards may be given for processes achieved by the group and for the quality and level of individual contributions. It may be possible to encourage the group to identify its own outcomes, assessment criteria and processes.

E-tivity actions

Be very specific about what you need your participants actually to do. I suggest you use verbs as instructions and invitations for the task. At Stages 1 to 3, I like the simple online verbs of 'post' and 'respond to' but there are many others.

However, participants' responses may be unpredictable. They may do a variety of things that you don't expect. I would consider almost any activity to be acceptable if it is consistent with task or group progress.

There are special aspects of working online that may interfere with active learning and which need to be taken into account in the design of the e-tivity task. The first is the role of emotions. Feelings such as frustration or anger are typically associated with the technology appearing not to work properly, or are affected by an incident with another participant or the e-moderator. Emotions associated with the technology and the e-moderating are commonest at Stages 1 and 2, and with relationships with other participants at Stages 3 and 4. By Stage 5, participants can usually handle both. Developing e-tivities that are appropriate for the stage in the model, whilst encouraging participants to acquire the skills to move up through the scaffolding, will help them to acquire skills in handling emotions.

Enable collaboration

When groups of learners get together, they nearly always exchange views and ideas. We know that people enjoy learning from the experiences of others as well as from resources such as websites and books. A key learning skill is shaping and achieving goals in learning sets or work teams. To offer these benefits, within any learning programme, a considerable amount of 'group work' needs to be included.

Traditionally, group work has been carried out with small face-to-face groups led by a tutor or instructor and hence often called 'tutorials'. The challenge is to ensure this happens equally well or better, in online encounters. E-tivities are the online equivalent of tutorials.

As you will have read so far, the ideas of e-tivities are based largely on participants making sense of learning material through interaction with their peers and with their e-moderators. This is why I always suggest that each e-tivity, at all stages of the model, includes a response to the messages of others to start to build participation. Without careful structuring, it is unlikely that discussion will move beyond, at best, sharing of information, support and encouragement (Jaques and Salmon, 2008).

As Chapter 2 suggests, it is important to establish group working gradually through the stages of the model. More in-depth learning in groups is then likely to happen at Stages 3 and 4. A broad distinction can be made between co-operative working (the group members help each other towards individuals' goals) and collaborative working (often linked with practice or knowledge construction, working together towards a group goal). Co-operation is often the aim at Stage 3 of the model; and collaboration, at Stage 4.

Collaboration requires an active sharing of information and intellectual resources amongst the participants. The best experience of collaboration by participants for learning purposes enables them to experience personal, individualistic, useful learning whilst contributing to a community of learners and the support and development of others. Never underestimate the resources that they work with: participants can comprehend, evaluate, debate, question, integrate and synthesize information online, with suitable e-tivities and ongoing support. One of the best ways of encouraging collaboration is around an inviting participative group task.

Over 100 theoretical models of group development are available (Jaques and Salmon, 2008). They all include four main characteristics: forming, control, work process and ending. One of the commonest models is Tuckman's forming, storming, norming, performing (Tuckman, 1965; Tuckman and Jenson, 1977). The five-stage model is a grounded model. It was developed through research with large numbers of students in the early days of online learning environments (see *E-moderating*, Salmon, 2011: Chapter 2). It was not a 'conversion' of processes described from face-to-face work groups. However, you will of course spot similarities. Some e-moderators find it helpful to explain the characteristics of successful team roles (for example, see Belbin, 1981) and then ensure that the main roles in the online group are taken up, such as chairing or convening, recording and timekeeping.

The role of the e-tivities designer is to state the purpose of the learning process and provide the environment to enable collaboration to take place in optimum conditions (rather than to do any of the collaborative work). With less experienced groups, it may be helpful, or necessary, for the e-moderator to set clear targets and deadlines for completion of sets of e-tivities and outputs, or to allow more time for the student group to work these out.

From Stage 4 onwards, e-moderators can design e-tivities that:

● create, define and identify a problem or opportunity associated with the desired learning outcome (e.g. working with a case study, analysing a situation, designing a product);
● identify team roles (though not necessarily allocating them);
● involve the team or group in working together to design analytical or other research, evaluation or enquiry activities and in carrying them out;
● involve the collaborative team in making choices and decisions;
● involve the collaborative team in creating and defending a plan or an action list;
● involve the collaborative team in presenting the outcomes to others outside the group, preferably through an online environment, and defending them;
● make appropriate time and space for reviewing and evaluating the learning.

Allow plenty of time for such processes.

Build in reflection

There are many ways to reflect. Some writers argue that reflection is essentially an independent activity. Other writers stress the importance of collaboration to the reflection process. Schön (1983) distinguishes between reflection on action (reflection after practice has been completed) and reflection in action (thinking that takes place in the midst of practice). I suggest you try out both reflection on action and reflection in action in your e-tivities and programmes, because both are valuable (Ross, 2012).

For example, the e-moderating courses at All Things in Moderation (www.atimod.com) offer a weekly 'point of learning' reflection opportunity (reflection in action). In addition, they offer a variety of opportunities for looking back and evaluating aspects of the dialogue during the last week of the course (reflection on action).

Many e-tivity designers first of all encourage participants to recall a familiar experience as a preparation for introducing them to a new one. The idea here is that previous experiences first need to be interrogated and challenged. Doing this increases creativity and avoids repeating unconscious assumptions. Flexibility in thinking is thus increased learning to better problem solving. Another key aspect of learning through reflective processes is that each adult learner will have different ways of dealing with ideas, using perhaps his or her own well-established learning approaches.

Reflection will be easier for some participants than others. Some people enjoy it very much; some prefer to 'push on'. However, as I think reflection is so important, I always include it as an essential activity. One point to emphasize: make it clear you are looking for participants' views, feelings, experiences and ideas. This is certainly one time when they can start their sentences with 'I'. But encourage them to end their message with a question or challenge to others, to encourage those others to reflect too.

As with all the e-tivities, I suggest you indicate why you are inviting participants to reflect. It's easy to pose a 'point of learning' reflective question at key times and ask participants to look back through the course regularly; invite them to respond to a simple question at the end of each session, once a week, and to the postings of others throughout. Also encourage them to revisit their own responses at any time. Almost all active participants express surprise, even amazement, when they glance back at what they have done, as the following examples show.

Seeing other points of view

I have tried on three different occasions to respond to this e-tivity, but each time I enter the forum, there is another person's reflections, which makes me think about my experience in a way not previously thought of. I think all the contributions to this section are interesting and thoughtful—that to respond to one is just not fair! NS

Recording emotions

Some interesting reflections posted for this e-tivity, and it is heartening to know that others are feeling the same as me—being an e-learner has made me see the other side of the coin. I have learned a lot about learning online—a whole range of emotions from feeling very lonely at times, experiencing happiness when I achieve something and guilt when I know I am not contributing as much as I should be. CH

More on e-tivity invitations—the precision

Few of us are really skilled at writing concise and effective instructions. The skill improves with practice and with feedback. It is particularly easy to create ambiguity in the task invitation. So I suggest that you test out your invitations on naive users, preferably potential participants (but if these are not available, then your colleagues or your children) to see what they make of them.

Try to ensure that all the information that participants need to post their first message in response is contained in one online message—and one screen if possible. You will see that I struggled a bit with Richard's first e-tivity design on pages 130–1—it's not easy to keep it all on one page.

Titles for e-tivities are very important. Think headlines. They should give information, invite individuals to take part, entice and distinguish one e-tivity from another. It's important to use numbers to indicate the stage of the model, the timing and the sequence of the e-tivities.

Incidentally, most online discussion forums take a title forward when participants reply (like e-mail), so the title you choose will probably appear many times and affect the online action. E-moderators should advise participants on the importance of careful titles, and about changing them in the headers of messages when topics change and develop. Participants expect the messages to contain roughly what they say in the title and may consider it impolite if they do not. It helps to create focus, and makes the e-moderators' job of weaving, archiving and summarizing much easier. You can be quite bossy about this!

E-tivity time

The use and experience of time is a major aspect of successful e-tivities. Time takes on a new dimension online, especially when working asynchronously and with numerous participants. Working asynchronously involves a radical rethink—not only of learning or teaching time but also of other aspects of life (Carmel and Espinosa, 2011). Some people find this very difficult indeed. By providing a clear indication that you expect active contribution and by pacing the e-tivity, you will help participants to make the adjustments to their lives. Your responsibility as the e-tivity designer is to provide regular activities that provide a framework—e-tivities that start and finish at predictable times and actions that occur regularly, such as the e-moderator's summary. In addition, you need to provide interest and motivation through underlying rhythm. Engaging in authentic tasks and working with others can provide this rhythm. Using clear start and finish times by the clock and the calendar enables synchronization and co-ordination of group activities. Such pacing needs to appear in the e-tivities because participants will not meet often enough online by chance to co-ordinate for themselves.

You and I frequently feel we do not have enough clock time: most people are very sensitive to being asked to engage in unproductive activities leading to a waste of time. If we focus on such a measurement of time, we can often become very alarmed about 'how much time' online learning is taking up. However, we all also know that we do not feel or experience time in the linear way a clock suggests. This is known as 'felt' time and it's linked directly to how connected we are to what we are doing. If we feel engaged and connected, then we focus less on time passing and experience time quite differently. If you are successful in building effective e-tivities, you may notice the reduction of the huge anxiety about the use of clock time.

Participants and their e-moderators will experience time in all sorts of ways when working online. One key aspect is the complexity associated with asynchronicity. Here is a little extract. It's from a novel and the author is describing a relationship that is developing based on an exchange of letters, but I think it illustrates the experience of asynchronicity most graphically:

> By the time you open a letter of mine and accept its truth, I am already somewhere else. When I read your letters, I am actually inside a moment of yours that has passed; I am with you inside a time you are no longer inhabiting. This works out to each of us being faithful to each other's abandoned moments.
>
> (Grossman, 2002, p. 107)

Remember that 'overfilling' an e-tivity is the enemy of active engagement online and the productive use of time. If you provide too many resources and too many questions, your participants will use them and have little time for each other. I find this is the commonest mistake and anxiety when working with university academics.

When designing e-tivities and providing invitations to take part, you need to take account of the time you expect participants to be online, responding both to your e-tivities invitations and to each other. It will be fairly easy to determine how long they may need to respond individually to your instructions. If necessary, you can get learners to test this. However, it's harder to tell how long they'll need to spend responding to each other. As a rough rule of thumb, I'd suggest that what might take a half an hour with a group of 10 face-to-face might take one week of elapsed time online, if each participant came back three times, read other people's messages and posted three of his or her own. The elapsed time is just as important as the actual online time, because participants may think a little about the e-tivities whilst going about their everyday tasks and engaging in 'reflection'.

It's really easy, when designing e-tivities, to imagine that participants are somehow in a 'bubble' that will enable them to focus on the e-tivity and give it their best attention—in other words, that they have distinctive time to give to their online learning. Have you noticed that, when you are working online, both family and colleagues interrupt you in a way they simply would not if you were in a face-to-face meeting or talking on the telephone? Research has shown that our working lives involve constant interruption. University, college or corporate participants may be in a learning resource centre or a library with other distractions, or they may be on a train or at an airport, where real linear time may interrupt their online time at any moment. As more and more of our participants access their learning resources and activities through mobile devices, the ability to multi-task becomes important.

A few learners (and e-moderators) are good at setting up their desks, mobiles and computers in such a way that they signal to the rest of the world, and to the people they live or work with, that they are fully engaged. But such people are rare.

You can productively try an e-tivity at Stage 1 that encourages sharing of ideas on avoiding distractions. But we need to see online e-tivity time as integrated as much as possible with everyone's lives and attention. Providing small discrete chunk of tasks helps, since these can be satisfying in themselves.

I have found that e-tivity designers and e-moderators have a strong tendency to underestimate the amount of time that is needed for achieving any one aspect of an e-tivity. In addition, and conversely, novice e-tivity designers frequently imagine quite long timescales with a multiplicity of complex e-tivities (see

Richard's first attempt in Chapter 1, pages 129–38). These are really hard to achieve successfully with asynchronous online groups. An elapsed time of 18 days overall, with paced e-tivities such as one individual response and one group response, is more probably realistic and successful in creating active engagement.

The most time-consuming aspect of e-moderating is making good summaries. However, summaries save a huge amount of participants' time, and increase learning and feedback. They are a particular boon to latecomers, who may otherwise be daunted by the number of messages awaiting them when they log on. Summaries can also provide an opportunity to encourage participants to contribute: if no one is prepared to offer a full summary, participants can be encouraged to offer one or two suggestions that the e-moderator can then build up into a summary (see Resources for Practitioners, pages 184–5).

I suggest that you develop e-tivities that address issues of working in online time from Stage 1 onwards. At Stages 3 and 4, creative e-moderators find ways of relating these to their discipline—such as science or literature.

Participants new to online learning always seem surprised about the use of their time:

I've enjoyed the week and am looking forward to the next. A fear or concern, however, is that of being in a constant state of catch-up. One of the problems I've had is that I log on to read the new messages and then come back later when I've thought of replies. By then everything has moved on. I guess this is driven by a fear of wanting to get 'the right answer' and having to spend time on a considered contribution. But I'm beginning to realize that it's the trying out of ideas that's important and that a supportive group is a good place to do that. MD

I am left uncomfortable at my intermittent presence caused by other commitments during this first week—I expect to be better organized after the next week. However, I have learned already the value of asynchronous discussion. I have been able to follow the e-tivities and its conversations even after extended absence. I may become less reactive in the near future! RC

I have the pleasure of doing this course in work time, but it is easy to get distracted by the everyday tasks . . . [I] log on as often as possible (ideally at least once a day), even if it is only for a short time. SC

I think the hardest thing so far has been finding time, always a tricky issue! Just skimming through messages is quick, but thinking about things and writing for the e-tivities is more time-consuming. I confess to doing the e-tivities but only responding to others in some not all of them. SH

All in all have enjoyed experience to date and look forward to getting down to some more proper discussion with everyone (am conscious have not 'met' all course members yet and would like to—must get up earlier!). HS

What about e-mod's time? Much more than you think. Needs discipline to say I won't keep logging on just to have another peek at how it's going . . . and then get totally carried away and time gets eaten up . . . Obviously it varies with the group—but academics are a case in point: they generate so many messages! (Says he, from bitter experience!) KG

Logging onto asynchronous courses in a regular rhythm—perhaps half an hour to an hour a day—seems most productive for most people and it is likely to be most conducive to reflection and the least intrusive to life in general. By developing a regular routine, you won't let the number of messages mount to a level that will cause you undue work when you log on.

Those with access from home and work, and whilst travelling, seem to make the fastest adjustments. That's a very good reason for making e-tivities available on personal mobile devices.

It's important to let colleagues at work, and/or family, know that when you're reading and typing on screen you are working and learning. Perhaps a little flag on the computer?

Create rhythm

To handle time for participants, the habit of regularly coming back online and taking part is important. We call this a sense of rhythm. All e-tivities should have built into them a pattern and a need for returning frequently.

In your e-tivities design you are aiming to:

- establish a pattern of online behaviour, of taking part and contributing;
- offer opportunities constantly for building on the work of others and receiving feedback;

- get people to start together and move on together;
- give them reasons and purposes for being online and for returning frequently;
- help them to develop a habit of coming back;
- include large numbers of small e-tivities—they work better than one or two daunting ones;
- provide occasional quizzes and opportunities, however small, for personal feedback from the e-moderator, which will help with pacing and rhythm.

Design for equity

Ensuring fairness and equality in online groups is a challenge for everyone involved (Dirckinck-Holmfeld, Hodgson and McConnell, 2012; Hodgson, 2008). Your e-tivity design can go a long way to promote active contributions and positive feelings. One way to start is to explore the way prejudice affects written and interactive communication.

Prejudices are a kind of emotional learning that occurs early in our lives. They are hard to eradicate, even in adults who feel they should not be prejudiced. The power of stereotypes in our minds is that they are largely self-confirming. We remember incidents that confirm our prejudices and forget those that discount them. This makes it hard to recognize prejudice in ourselves and to convince groups of the damage caused by them. So it is important to know as an e-tivities designer that you will have some deep-rooted and possibly subtly working prejudices. What you can do is to ensure that online behaviours—what you ask people to do and say—do not reinforce or act upon a stereotype.

Online, there are two particular issues that make it more likely that individuals will feel offended. First, everything that is 'said' is available for viewing and reviewing by everyone. Participants can therefore read many times something that might have offended. They may feel that they must respond because other people will otherwise have their prejudices reinforced. Second, there is a lack of tone and body language in 'Netspeak', the words people use online. Sometimes intention and meaning are conveyed less accurately than in face-to-face encounters, particularly by inexperienced participants.

These problems are relatively uncommon. Most online participants are careful, reflective and supportive of each other. However, we should not turn away from potential discrimination in our groups, because the learning of individuals and of the whole group may suffer. Humour also needs to be used with care. The wider the cultural mix or the scaling up of your e-tivities, the more likely it is that a participant will be offended. What is considered humour is very diverse.

I quote here from a short online course for educators learning to undertake e-tivities design:

20 November

From: Marion Martin (participant)
If I am feeling a bit down I sometimes have a look at uglypeople. com as it makes me laugh! I would use the ugly people website to use as a spark to encourage students to post something—at Stage 2 for socializing.

21 November
From: Daniel Sanders (e-moderator)

Hi Marion, thanks for this opportunity to disagree on a subject that might be sensitive for some participants. Since we don't know what any of our participants look like (unless they have sent a picture) and looks are rather subjective anyway, there may be a danger of some of us feeling that we look like one of the people featured on the site. This might generate feelings that may be hard for some to express online, thus putting some in a position where they are uncertain how to respond.

In working with your students, I suggest that any sensitive topics are left until the group feels comfortable enough to challenge each other's contributions.

What do others think? Daniel

21 November
From: Cecily Smith (participant)

Marion, I concur with Daniel's words of caution! We have no idea whether our course participants have physical disabilities or irregularities that they have been teased about. On the other hand, given my sense of humour, I actually found the site a bit of a laugh. I guess that humour is something that is shared between people who know each other fairly well and therefore has the potential to backfire, especially online.

Whenever I quote sites to people I try to give them a short précis about what the site contains. Then they can decide whether they actually want to visit it. Mind you, I am sure you are thinking that Ugly.com is pretty self-explanatory. Cheers Cecily

22 November
From: Hannah Sparm (participant)

Daniel Sanders writes: 'I suggest that any sensitive topics are left until the group feels comfortable enough to challenge each other's contributions. What do others think?' I felt quite threatened when two of the participants from this group seemed to disagree with me in e-tivity 3.4, so I hesitate to reply to this as I don't want to upset Marion; however, I think the issue is important. I felt that the website is an unkind one. I have a very dear friend who has been suicidal. She feels that she is fat and that everyone despises her for it. She has a beautiful Ferrari but finds it difficult to get out of the car at petrol stations for the fear that people will think 'Nice car, shame about the driver.' From previous discussions we have had, I know that she would be mortified to see this website.

I have learnt hugely from your thoughtful contributions to the e-tivities, Marion, so please forgive me when I say that I think that this is not a good avenue to pursue.

With very best wishes, Hannah

23 November
From: Marion Martin (participant)

Many apologies to everyone who found the website not the most appropriate. On reflection, it was poor judgement on my part.

Colleagues, you bring a valuable lesson in understanding the nature of this medium and I think all your points were valid. I found the nature and tone of your comments very supportive and it made me realize that humour is a very personal choice.

However, it has some positive outcomes: contributions have been challenged; and a valuable lesson has been learnt (by me for the future). Although I sit downhearted as I write this, supportive comments from the group have been gratefully received and acknowledged, which still make me feel as an accepted and valued member of the group.

Thanks, Marion

Numbers of participants

Smallish groups work most easily online. This is unsurprising, because each individual comes to know other members of the group quicker and more easily: each is encouraged to contribute actively and more sustained engagement is thus achieved. I find that groups of 12 to 20 participants work really well. They can be successfully divided into smaller groups and put together again within e-tivity processes. They can manageably work together and then contribute to bigger plenary processes.

I usually appoint one trained part-time e-moderator for groups up to 20, with well-structured e-tivities. I have two e-moderators working together for larger groups or (preferably) I divide participants into groups of 20 with an e-moderator each. With well-designed e-tivities, e-moderators can handle two or three groups each. With these numbers, e-moderators can be effective and experience work satisfaction, and burnout is avoided.

With larger groups there is a risk that individuals will not participate because they see that others have already made the point they wish to make. The greater volume of messages tends to put off all but the most active participants, and lurking and vicarious learning are common. However, the way to involve bigger groups and larger number of participants is very regular archiving and summarizing of messages—even daily if necessary. See Resources for Practitioners 20.

There are also risks with small groups. With a group of, say, only six, if one or two participants drop out for any reason, those that are left behind feel bereft and put-upon, and the group may have too few members to be self-sustaining.

One word of warning. You need to be very specific about who is in which group in your e-tivity invitational message. Unlike in face-to-face situations, where participants can quickly and easily sort themselves into groups, it is possible to waste a week just getting into teams online. The easiest way is to specify the maximum size of each group and fill them up on the basis of the sequence of their arrival. When a group reaches a specified size, then start another. Or you might also use criteria such as month of birth or surnames. If you want to form groups based on prior checks or tests, then allow extra time. Of course, as participants reach Stage 4 e-tivities, they may be better able to organize themselves online.

Stories from the front line 4

Sue Kokonis, Director of Teaching for Swinburne Online, tells us about her experience of designing for groups in entirely online e-tivity-based courses.

At Swinburne Online we work with online groups of 25 students. We call our e-moderators 'e-learning advisors'. They are trained and developed in weaving and summarizing, giving effective feedback and encouraging engagement. We allocate four hours per e-learning advisor per week over the 12-week semester to each participant cohort of 25. We know the time commitment is higher in the earlier steps of the five-stage model.

We find that the participation in e-tivities somewhat ebbs and flows within each group, with particularly quiet times observed just after a large assessment, as students catch their breath! So weaving, summarizing and feedback work fluctuates too.

Design for lower costs

Some organizations believe that they can obtain a better return on their investment in e-learning by disposing entirely of lecturer, trainer or e-moderating costs. From the rest of this book, you will see that I think that discarding human intervention is neither appropriate nor successful. Enormous value is added to the participant experience by skilled e-moderation. However, structured, paced and carefully constructed e-tivities reduce the amount of e-moderator time, and directly affect satisfactory learning outcomes, adding value to the investment. From the start of e-learning, it was recognized that costs are reduced by appropriate online pedagogy (Ash and Bacsich, 2002).

E-tivities take time to design properly and require 'space' and experimentation. However, one designer can create an e-tivity that can be used by many groups, either in parallel or over time. It is important to build in the reduction of e-moderator interaction time through the design of the e-tivities. Avoid suggesting that the e-moderator should respond to every student posting.

Skilled and trained e-moderators can often handle large numbers of students online, if well-constructed e-tivity programmes are used. Using other people to support participants, such as graduate students or alumni of the five-stage model, often helps. At Stages 1 to 3, the e-moderator will need to spend a fair amount of time getting the e-tivities going. At Stages 4 and 5, he or she can log on less often, but achieving good plenaries, feedback and summaries can be demanding. The effort should go into these for greatest impact on the learning.

There seems to be an overall optimum point on costs at around 30 or 40 participants to one e-moderator (Rumble, 2010). Most well-designed e-tivities run successfully with a ratio of up to 20 participants to one e-moderator, so have one (well-trained) e-moderator running two or more groups for optimum cost–benefit.

Once e-tivities are designed and built into a programme, the key issue is the cost of arranging appropriate e-moderator support. The better designed the e-tivities are, the clearer the instructions, the less the need for constant human intervention. Develop systems for reuse, recycling and sharing of e-tivities' invitational messages. Choose technologies that will allow you to upscale as rapidly as possible, ones that can be expanded free or cheaply, and add in social media (see Chapter 4).

There's more in *E-moderating* (Salmon, 2011) about reducing the costs of the e-moderators, and see Resources for Practitioners 3, pages 125–8 for open educational resources as sparks.

Write invitations

The heart of understanding both writing and taking part in text-based communication is grounded in 'Netspeak'. The way people communicate online is a unique and evolving mix of written and spoken communication. In on-screen text messages, people tend to write as if they were talking (Crystal, 2004). Think about the huge variety of talking styles there are. And many people are now familiar with communicating in all sorts of ways through social media and through mobile devices.

However, your written invitations to e-tivities need to be completely clear. It is important to be brief both in your stimulus and in your invitations—no more than one screen—and to indicate clearly the kind of brevity you expect in response. This is very challenging, but essential if you are to avoid obscurity and ambiguity. Think in terms of the number of sentences in a response, the length of sentences and the amount of text on the screen.

I promise you will get better with practice, and especially if you design with others or check out your draft e-tivities before you launch them in your programme (see Resources for Practitioners 24, pages 202–3).

Online messages, even well-planned ones, can very easily be ambiguous or misinterpreted. E-moderators do not have quite the same opportunity for spontaneously putting participants right (or back) on track as a face-to-face facilitator does. Be prepared, during the e-tivity event itself, for directions to be taken that are unexpected or for e-tivities to be challenged in various ways (this is especially likely to happen from Stage 3 onwards). Be prepared to go with the flow. Be prepared for changes the next time the e-tivity is run.

Resources for Practitioners 12, pages 166–7 explores 'Netspeak' a little more.

Concentrate on inviting online actions and state what behaviour is expected of participants during the e-tivity. Be very specific about what you need your participants to do. I suggest you use verbs as invitations to the task.

Providing sparks to start the dialogue

Knowledge involves thinking with information. Participants do not start completely 'cold', but start with some information or knowledge. So, for e-tivities you need to decide what information will be provided as a starting point—the spark to begin the process of group learning and knowledge construction. The e-tivity designer presents an issue: a dilemma, problem, challenge or model. Use different kinds of data and information, but keep spark paragraphs and links short. If appropriate, you may well wish to provide references, further reading or illustrative links, but try to avoid making any of these necessary for active engagement in the online task.

There are many types of sparks for e-tivities. The main types provide a small piece of information, a model, concept or example to which participants can react, or ask for views, information or experiences. You might also find a trigger from what participants bring to the e-tivity. Consider what they bring, what their interests may be, what kind of content will interest them, what kinds of activities they will want to be engaged in. Provide variety throughout the programme and the sequence. Use available resources as sparks wherever possible (see Resources for Practitioners 3, pages 125–8).

Avoid filling the invitational message with a whole variety of different spark materials, references or links. If you want to provide sparks with more difficulty, depth or breadth, build them into separate e-tivities.

Chapter 4

Choices

The technology spectrum

This book's companion website (e-tivities.com) provides many links to all the platforms described in this chapter, and new ones as they become available. The 20 suggestions here have been tried for e-tivities. We don't know enough yet to be able to suggest which are more important or 'best'. I've just indicated the places to start, that I know have worked for some designers and e-moderators in practice.

The concept of e-tivities started with text-based asynchronous forums or bulletin boards. Asynchronous text-based forums were what I had available at the time . . . and they are still highly accessible and good to deploy for low-cost, high-value learning activities. Text and dialogue continue to be the primary ways of creating learning with others (Bonk and Zhang, 2008), but there are many more technologies now with different functions and characteristics (Jewitt, 2006). If you are experienced with e-tivities, I'm sure you are already using a wider variety of platforms for sparks or participation, so you might just like to skim this chapter. If you are starting out or need some refreshing, this is for you.

We have a plethora of new choices. The advent of social media and the contributing web has hugely raised the awareness of technology as offering new forms of promoting interaction and participation (Preece and Shneiderman, 2009)—something e-tivity designers and successful e-moderators always knew. Many of the examples I suggest have been used for news, marketing campaigns or individual notifications to the world, but here I note how they have been used for e-tivities and learning groups.

To make an informed choice among them, you need to understand the technology's characteristics and you need to try them first for yourself. For many of the platforms that are about co-operation and collaboration, you'll need to set up a sympathetic group of people for the trial. One good way of thinking about the wide variety of options is considering them all as environments for learning, offering different opportunities and tending to promote certain kinds of group behaviour (Wenger *et al.*, 2009).

You also need to think about how to combine the use of different technological opportunities—what is usually called blended learning (Littlejohn and Pegler, 2007). For some people this term means a variety of kinds of activity; for others it means a mixture of face-to-face or on-campus learning with online learning. E-tivities work in both kinds. A more up-to-date definition still is how learning designers are creating what they call 'seamless' environments—so that learners can move without difficulty from their mobile devices, to their laptops, to the workplace or other learning locations and sometimes to the campus.

When you design your e-tivities, try to find out about the special characteristics of the software and platform available to your learners and exploit them to the utmost! Once the e-tivities are running and people are taking part, however, let your knowledge of these characteristics slip into the background. In this way, the technology should enable learning without de-motivating learners or becoming a focus of attention in itself. After all, we can expect few of the participants to be captivated by the technology and software: rather, they are likely to see these as a means leading to better experiences and achievement.

More portable and life-integrated e-tivities

Mobile learning offers three key features to enhance learning that are of great value in e-tivities: authenticity, collaboration and personalization (Kearney, Shuck, Burden and Aubusson, 2012).

There are five main ways of designing e-tivities so that participants really benefit from portable devices with learning resources and connections.

One way is to provide regular learning resources and interaction for participants in such a way that they can access and continue to take part in any spare moments in their lives. Resources can be downloaded and easily carried around if participants have intermittent networking opportunities.

Another design option is to have participants engage in reflection and communication with others at a critical moment of thought or learning. It's worth building e-tivities that exploit your participants' mobility and their many locations as they move around in their daily lives.

The third way is the juxtaposition of reality and virtuality. This includes visiting ancient societies that no longer exist, journeying to the moon, taking part in activities or visits that would be unsafe in real life, or practising medical or scientific procedures unavailable or inappropriate in real life. In such ways we can maximize learning experiences.

The fourth is to use, as sparks, the continuing array of excellent mobile applications (apps) available on Apple and Android devices. These include those developed for learning, plus many others developed for fun or business that can be harnessed for learning and teaching purposes.

The fifth is augmented reality, which means supplementing the view of physical, real-world environments by computer-mediated sound, video, graphics or GPS data. Increasingly, augmented reality will become lower in cost and more available for learning.

As always, make your choice depending on the purpose of the e-tivity and the accessibility for the participants.

As I write, nearly all of the technology examples I suggest for e-tivities are available when a hand-held device is attached to a wireless network. Some then look rather different than they do on a website, some work better and a few, where very high or fast bandwidth is required, don't work at all. But by the time you read my comments this may have changed. And it will go on changing. Try the examples for yourself before you design e-tivities.

Technology availability: institutionally supported platforms

In educational institutions and many other organizations, some kind of learning management system (LMS) or virtual learning environment (VLE) is provided. These systems are secure, backed up, supported, have help desks and offer a variety of options and functions for e-tivities. I've used the term 'LMS/VLE' throughout the book—different names for more or less the same kind of platform are used in different countries. There are commercial ones, such as Blackboard and Desire2Learn, and open source ones, such as Moodle. Your organization will have invested considerable financial and human resources in the LMS/VLE and will want you to try it first. It will certainly have an asynchronous bulletin board, a place to make announcements and post your e-tivity invitations. Check out whether it offers basic tools and whether you have access to add-ons such as wikis, e-portfolios and synchronous virtual classrooms. There are benefits if everything needed for participants to take part is in one place and behind one password. So make the very most of what you have got! If you choose other platforms and processes, make links from within the LMS/VLE to them.

The rest of the (e-)world

There are many environments, tools and applications that are not owned, nor can be, by an educational organization.

There are challenges. You are unlikely to get formal support from within your own organization and will need to rely on information from elsewhere. The provider might be in another time zone and you may have to rely on e-mail. There are some risks for example, uncertainty when a down-time may occur. However, many educational technologists and their communities offer considerable informal support and help to others.

You may need to ask what exactly is happening to your participants' data and contributions, and that of your own. You may want to remove your data or make sure the learning group secures it when you've finished the e-tivities. Countries have different policies and laws and, for some, where the data is held is an issue.

Quite commonly, the owners and providers of these tools will support themselves by advertising through the platform or application (app). Or, if you prefer, you can often avoid advertising by paying something and perhaps securing a helpline. Sometimes you will need to take out a paid subscription. If you pay you usually get extended features and more availability. In many online games you may need to buy items to progress or secure more features. Costs are usually low. Look for or ask for educational discounts.

Most applications and platforms outside your institution's LMS/VLE require registration by the users, so you'll need to explain to participants exactly how to do this. Even if participants are already users of a platform, they may prefer to create a new account for the purpose of working with the learning group and doing e-tivities. Always offer this option.

Some newer Web 2.0 tools do come and go, so are less secure. These days there's usually some warning of their likely disappearance. But it's a good idea to regularly warn participants to save any critical unrepeatable work.

Some applications and platforms have ways of creating private or bounded groups for a purpose: for example, Facebook offers this facility. You'll want to do this for your e-tivities, I'm sure.

There are so many options around, it shouldn't matter too much which you choose; just make sure everything is accessible to your participants, preferably both on fixed computers and mobiles. If you are dealing with large numbers of participants, you might want to stick to platforms that do not require the very latest system to access them.

Some platforms provide a suite of applications and platforms, which, if you have some skills, you could put together to provide a LMS/VLE-like environment. I'd start by looking at the Google suite. Try searching for 'Google apps for educators'. It's worth considering using some of these platforms in addition to your institution's LMS/VLE. At the time I write, many more students voluntarily engage with publicly available social network services than institutionally provided online education tools (Flavin, 2012; Jones, Gaffney-Rhys and Jones, 2011).

Considering the choices

I strongly recommend that you get your overall plan designed first through a storyboard, which includes learning outcomes and assessment (see Chapter 5).

- First remind yourself of the purpose of the e-tivity or series of e-tivities and how it/they fit with the overall objectives or learning outcomes.
- Then consider the stage in the scaffold and the level of skill and competence your participants have in order to enable them to take part, contribute and benefit.
- Be ambitious—the technologies that follow are already in use for business, communication, entertainment or informal learning, so can more easily be 'translated' for teaching and learning.
- Then consider what key piece of core or threshold knowledge or interaction (Meyer and Land, 2005) you wish to focus on for this particular e-tivity or sequence.
- Now decide whether you are looking mainly for a spark. If so, then first set about finding open educational resources, rather than becoming diverted to writing or producing the materials for yourself. See Resources for Practitioners 3.
- If you are planning for specific types of interaction, participation or contribution to take place, perhaps to solve a pedagogical problem or encourage more engagement, then take a moment to consider what kind of technological functionality will make this easier, faster or better.

Now you can move on to the technology beyond the bulletin board or forum

I've divided these suggestions into those that provide SPARKS AND CONTRIBUTIONS and those for WORKING TOGETHER. In the first group are platforms and applications with a range of interactive features and functions. In the second are platforms and applications that can start participation and dialogue, or that offer accessible repositories for participants to store, view and respond to each others' contributions.

There are many other ways of people working and learning together, e.g. through gesture-based gaming networked environments such as Xbox or the Wii, but I've not tried using the e-tivities structure with them and haven't (yet) come across anyone who has. So if you try e-tivities with any platform not suggested here, please let me know. There will be space for new types of technologies for e-tivities on the Web and Facebook sites linked to this book.

My categorizations here are blunt instruments. They are based on the technologies' relevance and use for e-tivities. Many platforms and environments offer opportunities for interesting forms of participation, creative sparks and combinations of them and many others besides. For example, e-tivity designers could use existing pre-created 'recommendations' sites as a spark, or an e-tivity could be around creating one, as an individual or as a group, which is then in a working together category, but could also become a spark for the next e-tivity. So my suggestions are starters: be creative and report back, please!

Feast on these 10 technologies for working together

1 Wikis

Examples: Wikispaces, Mediawiki, PBWorks, Googlesites.

A wiki is a website that allows its participants to add, modify or delete its content via a Web browser or mobile app. Participants contribute text or attach images. Most LMS/VLEs have them and there are many others available in the Cloud. Many wikis permit control over who can do what on the wiki site. Editing rights for individuals may permit changing, adding or removing material.

Wikis are good for working together, with most kinds of e-tivities. The output or summary can be used as a spark for the next e-tivity. They call for a low level of technical and pedagogical skills for design and from participants and e-moderators.

Wikis have proved exceptionally valuable in e-tivities delivery, but you must provide the structure for responses—otherwise, they grow too quickly and become complex and confusing. They enable participants to respond easily to a spark, and then respond to others. Participants seem to write quite a lot in wikis, but e-moderators find they are easy and quick to weave, add feedback to and summarize. It's a good idea to provide some structure for responses—such as a table—to avoid words appearing all over the place. It's easy to monitor how individual participants are contributing: wikis keep track of who edited what and when.

2 Voice boards

Examples: Wimba Voice Board, VoiceThread, Vocaroo.

Voice boards are asynchronous, like online discussion boards; contributors post responses with their voices through little audio messages (rather than text). Once participants get the hang of it, it can be quite quick to post.

Voice boards can accommodate most kinds of e-tivities: they help with group forming and feedback, since the human voice adds tone and warmth, or where spoken words are important, e.g. language learning. Try them for one or two e-tivities after participants and e-moderators are familiar with the text-based asynchronous forums. The use of tone and emotion in the human voice seems to promote interest and participation.

Like wikis, the boards call for a low level of technical and pedagogical skills for design and from participants and e-moderators. You can use audio only for these types of e-tivities or you can use audio and text.

Use a voice board that offers threaded discussions to keep track of responses. The boards are currently a little harder and take longer for the e-moderator to weave and summarize because each post needs to be opened and listened to. Always suggest that each audio posting has a short descriptive title or line or two as to its content—this helps.

Most regular discussion forums offer the opportunity to attach an audio or video file to an individual message or posting. It's not quite the same as a voice board but you might like to experiment that way first.

3 Blogs

Examples: WordPress, Blogger, Edublogs.

Blogs are good for sharing and presenting information and views, practising contributing online, reflecting at the point of learning, and for online and academic writing. They call for a low level of skills from participants and e-moderators, but a medium level from designers, because a bit of setting up is needed.

Blogs work like a diary published on the Web. They provide an easy way of documenting learning thoughts and outcomes. Participants' entries can include text, images and links. Typically these entries are displayed in reverse chronological order. They offer the opportunity for comments and feedback from others. They can be open to all or restricted to a group.

Blogs are used in many courses, mainly for personal or group reflections on e-tivities. You can invite comments from the learning group. Blogs are great for looking back at various points in the course, for revision, promoting reflection and revisiting portions of the course before assessment. They are also a good way for e-moderators to give personal or group feedback.

4 Micro-blogs

Examples: Twitter, Tumblr, Plurk.

Micro-blogs are like blogs but feature very short entries. For example, on Twitter, posts are limited to 140 typed characters, so it's like blogging, but smaller and faster.

Micro-blogs are good for working together and generating sparks. They can provide quick interactive e-tivity responses and surveys. A summary of a micro-blogging e-tivity is good as a spark to lead into the next topic. Although writing such short messages takes a little practice, micro-blogs demand little in the way of skills from designers, participants or e-moderators. You could say they promote concise writing!

There is a 'tagging' system so that entries can be grouped easily. Hashtags can be used to define your learning groups or a community, particularly around an event, course or topic, and are easily used by the e-moderator or by participants to collect entries together.

Micro-blogs are very low cost and widely accessible for participants on any network. They are good for quickly sharing information with a wider audience and receiving speedy responses. Participants can then post questions and respond, and others can similarly review, reply, comment, or tick the 'like' box on the post. Micro-blog entries may include photos and links.

5 Text messages on mobile phones

Text messages are familiar to almost everyone; they may be short and up to 140 characters on many mobile devices, and work with 3G access when the Internet is unavailable. They demand little in the way of design skills, from participants and e-moderators, though group texting will probably require a subscription service.

Text messages can link e-tivities to real-world practice or experience. They can be used by participants who are dispersed with low levels of, or intermittent access to, the Internet and/or with simple mobile phones. They can be valuable when participants need to be in a workplace or on field work whilst responding.

You will find them particularly useful when sharing ideas, running quick surveys (e.g. collecting real data on the fly and reporting it), or with small peer groups collecting and reporting field data. Use text messages also for reminders, updates and peer support. You will have to be quick with e-moderating to maintain focus and interest—it's not so easy to cut and paste into a Word document for summarizing, which is usually important for e-moderating feedback. If participants have smart mobile devices, you can embed links or share pictures and videos via the messaging function. If you want to try sharing multi-media files and keep costs down, take a look at whatsapp.com.

6. Multi-user games

Example: World of Warcraft, Camelot: Battle for the North.

Most of these games are based on complex logistics and have interesting multi-media features, as well as communications devices. They are good for working together, experiencing online group work, exploring online identities, experiencing competition, co-operation and collaboration, establishing strong coalitions, understanding logistics and consequences and giving and receiving feedback and support.

You may be wondering, however, about the skills needed. If you use commercially produced games, the games are all set up for you. You will need some creativity to link the games to your learning outcomes. The demands on e-moderators are medium-level: the e-moderator needs to practise the game, and become familiar with its features and quirks, to be able to help participants to play successfully.

Game participants can behave co-operatively or competitively. The game will set certain objectives but the group can also creatively make their own. Take breaks from the game for e-tivities outside the games environment to discuss what's going on, raise and reinforce learning points and smooth any ruffled feathers.

7 Three-dimensional multi-user virtual worlds

Examples: Second Life, OpenSim.

In immersive environments such as these virtual worlds, participants can explore ways of living and learning that are not available in real life. These worlds are particularly good for role-playing, problem solving and simulation e-tivities. Participants can establish identities as avatars, work together in authentic ways and engage in scenario-based, immersive learning activities.

Some design skills are needed to create suitable immersive environments, although many can be 'found', free or at very low cost. Participants and e-moderators need to create or acquire avatars and must develop in-world skills such as moving around and making gestures. It is easy to make recordings and take pictures that can be used as sparks. The five-stage model and e-tivities have been researched and they work well in virtual worlds: if you're interested, please read Salmon (2009) and Salmon, Nie and Edirisingha (2010). There are also virtual world case studies and advice in *E-moderating* (Salmon, 2011).

8 Synchronous virtual classroom

Examples: Collaborate, Adobe Connect, Live Meeting, Wizid.

Clearly these are good for working together, for holding lectures, seminars and tutorials where participants are remote and scattered. They also work well with some distributed participants and some participants who are co-located in a physical classroom. They have many of the presentation features of a face-to-face session, including interactive tools such as voting, and make similar demands on design and delivery skills. They work well where most other e-tivities are asynchronous: you can use them to indicate the end of one step in the five-stage model and to encourage participants to move on together as a cohort. Simpler forms (such as Skype, which offers audio conferencing) also work well.

Ensure that participants have prepared their computers and practised in advance—most synchronous virtual classrooms require up-to-date software and a lack of it can be an annoying barrier if left until the seminar starts.

E-moderators, it's very common for small things to go wrong. Unlike with asynchronous forums, there's no time to go off and get help. For the first few times I suggest you have technical support or a more experienced user with you. If you are presenting, planning for interactivity is essential: load up slides or links in advance, get the sound working, but try to avoid presenting long lectures. With any kind of 'presentation' the visuals need to change frequently and there should be pauses every five minutes or so for feedback and to answer questions.

Participants can contribute via polls, quizzes, or take over the presentation and share resources and desktops. The e-moderator needs to be familiar with moderating in synchronous environments and be prepared to multi-task fairly intensively (there's more on this in Salmon, 2011). If you are presenting information, it's a good idea to have someone else e-moderate the chat box, summarize questions for you, alert you to other functions, such as 'raised hands' or 'clapping'. Participants can share their work with each other and receive peer and e-moderator feedback. Offer small 'rooms' for break-out groups so smaller group interaction is possible.

9 Mind and concept mapping

Examples: MindMeister, SpicyNodes, iMindMap, Cacoo, MindManager, FreeMind, Cmap (for concept mapping), bubbl.us (for brainstorming), Prezi (for mind mapping and presentation functions).

These tools are for Web-based visual thinking, 'mapping' and planning. They offer ways of visually structuring and developing thoughts, ideas and understandings and easily sharing them. They are useful in encouraging group note taking, sharing and revising e-tivities.

Mind maps usually deploy a spider diagram format with 'legs' emerging from a central topic. Concept mapping offers more flexible structures and typically demands that you specify the nature of links between concepts or nodes. They can be combined with real-time text chat to help the maps emerge, and participants' own images can be inserted. They demand only low levels of skills in design and delivery.

They are good for structuring understanding, explaining, problem deconstruction, revising, planning and online collaboration, especially at Stage 4 of the five-stage model. They can encourage pairs or trios to capture each other's ideas and to give and receive feedback and verification.

You can use them for encouraging collaboration in e-tivities. They may appeal especially to more visual participants or systems thinkers. Be warned, however, that they become chaotic if more than around 10 take part in one mapping activity.

10 Social networking

Examples: Facebook, LinkedIn, Ning, FriendFeed, Yammer.

Social networking is useful for making announcements, getting to know about others, crossing disciplines, easily commenting, giving quick feedback to others, finding shared interests and encouraging networking and collaboration. LinkedIn is good for students starting on job searches, and has a more professional feel than Facebook.

You will need medium-level design and delivery skills. If you already use Facebook for family and friends, you might want to set up a separate identity in your role as an e-moderator, and encourage participants to do so if they wish. You'll need to prepare a course group site for the e-tivities. It's pretty easy, but allow yourself a bit of time. Often participants become self-supporting quite quickly in these environments, so negotiate how often the e-moderator needs to go in. One note of warning: social networking is not secure and there can be problems regarding ownership of data.

Now have a look at 10 technologies which are good for sparks and contributions.

11 Crowd-driven wikis

Examples: Wikipedia, Formspring.

Besides being open and free, Wikipedia sites are stable. Most are kept reasonably fluid and up-to-date, some very frequently. They are easy to embed in e-tivities as a link. They demand low level skills in design and delivery.

Use them where you want participants to compare and contrast, or to evaluate different types of information. They are good for looking back for hindsight and insight . . . to lead to foresight. Point out the nature of Creative Commons licensing (see Resources for Practitioners 3, pages 125–8) and how such crowd-driven knowledge can be used and evaluated.

12 Social bookmarking

Examples: Delicious, Diigo, Symbaloo, Springpad, Pinterest, Mendeley.

These offer a way of organizing and presenting Web links. They are good for sparks and contributions because participants can use them for finding, collecting, aggregating, tagging and sharing Web-based resources. They call for low levels of skills in design and delivery.

They are great for encouraging students to find and contribute resources of all kinds and then explore and evaluate those offered by others. Use them when participants are at Stages 2 and 3 of the five-stage model to encourage steps towards group working around a topic.

13 Recommendations and contributions

Examples: Scoop.it, Pinterest.

There are sites on practically any topic you can imagine. They are generated by contribution and filtered either collaboratively, based on lists of preferences of users (recommenders), or by the topics. They provide a smorgasbord of themes and items to explore. Participants create, find, construct lists, curate, share and present resources.

These are good for collaborative activities that involve building options and preferences, comparing selections, compiling list of sites for presentation and evaluation by others. Design and delivery are easy: as an e-moderator you do need skills when it comes to teaching about crowd sourcing and evaluation of knowledge.

14 Massive contributions and collections

Examples: Flickr (images), YouTube (videos), SlideShare (presentations), SoundCloud (audio), Khan Academy (educational video), Kickstarter (entrepreneurial ideas). There are also sites for displaying portfolios of creative work, e.g. Dribbble for designers, Behance for art work.

These are brilliant for finding interesting, fun, different content and media to liven up e-tivities. It is easy to search and make links without registering. To contribute, upload and set up groups you need to register, but design and delivery require few skills.

Use these technologies for finding interesting sparks when designing e-tivities. The websites are good for encouraging evaluation and comparison e-tivities and for enabling understanding of the nature of reuse and permissions of found resources. Individuals or groups of participants can make their contributions, or they can work together to produce output and results for peer review or for formative or summative assessment.

15 Syndication and update

Examples: Google Reader or Trapit, exploiting RSS. Applications like Trapit report on results from regular searches of the Internet for topics you have specified, using RSS protocols.

RSS (rich site summary, or really simple syndication) provides a 'feed'—it's a way of automatically enabling you to stay constantly aware of Web-published material in your relevant field by alerting you to new material. RSS feeds can be read using software called an RSS reader. The way the link is generated through the RSS reader can appear in many different ways—text or more visual.

These provide relevant, immediately updated RSS feeds for your topic into your LMS/VLE site or into individual e-tivities. You can use them for e-tivities that teach skills in evaluating and applying information found. They are good for sparks in e-tivities because they are constantly updated.

You might need a bit of technical help to set up the RSS feeds for the most relevant stuff: both design and delivery demand medium-level skills.

16 Document collaboration

Examples: Google Docs, Microsoft Sky Drive, Zoho, MoPad, DropBox.

All of these are good for sparks and contributions. They encourage and enable synchronous or asynchronous collaboration on a written document and then storage. They also have chat, drawing and charting functions. They are for groups working together on data collection, brainstorming and writing projects. Some of these sites work similarly to a wiki. Some are easier than others to export for e-mailing or printing.

Document collaboration works well with co-located or dispersed participants. Participants' drafts are easy to e-moderate and give feedback on, or they can keep them private. More ambitious writing-based e-tivities might lead to a jointly produced report or book, perhaps openly published (check out Wikibooks).

As a designer, you need medium-level skills to put some structure into the website so you avoid very confused documents. For delivery, the software is pretty easy to use, though the multiple authorship feels a little strange until you get used to it.

17 Random discovery

Example: StumbleUpon.

These platforms are good for sparks and contributions because they prompt new ideas and creativity, making links across disciplines and concepts. They require only low-level design and delivery skills. Once set up, they deliver randomized Web-based resources of all kinds at a click.

At Stages 1 and 2 in the five-stage model, random discovery works well for sharing and fun activities when you want to encourage participants to work together.

18 E-portfolios

Examples: PebblePad, Mahara.

E-portfolios created by learners are a collection of digital artefacts articulating and presenting learning (both formal and informal) experiences and achievements. These encourage group collaboration and are valuable for maintaining evidence over long periods as well as for presentations of experience. Again, they require only low-level design and delivery skills, but you may find that it isn't always easy to get participants to keep their portfolios going or to effectively embed these into their e-tivities work. Encourage them to reflect at key points in their e-tivities sequence and to provide evidence of their participation and learning. If the e-portfolios are maintained, they can become a permanent record and a showcase of a learner's journey and achievements.

The software provides for the collection of electronic evidence, in multiple formats, that can be assembled and managed, protected by private passwords but shareable. E-portfolios are a way of providing evidence of output of learning and achievement and a platform for self-expression. They can be maintained dynamically over time. Check whether you want one that participants can 'take with them' after the e-tivity or the course, or after they qualify—or a lighter version may do, and ask them whether parts of the e-portfolio can at least be opened up to their learning group or community as well as the e-moderator.

19 Mobile apps

Examples: thousands of examples available for Apple, Windows and Android.

These can be used for collaboration, finding resources, understanding, analysing, creating and presenting, virtual experience, and so on. With thousands of apps available, many setting out to educate and others to entertain, communicate or inform, these are good for sparks and contributions, and demand only low-levels skills.

You should be wary of low, quality apps. Before you go looking, check the pedagogical purpose you have in mind. Try the apps before you buy, recommend or embed in e-tivities. In the e-tivities, make clear to participants why you have included the ones you choose.

20 Location-based imaging

Examples: Google Earth, Google Street View, Android Footprints.

This imaging is good for sparks arising from exploration (virtual journeys) and sharing. It calls for low-level skills. Virtual globe mapping, imaging and geographical information platforms are easy to use. Many 3-D views are now available and the software is constantly improved.

Though there are obvious uses in e-tivities for geography-related disciplines, this technology is also great fun and powerful, as participants share visual information, leading to sharing and discovery.

I'm sure there's something here for everyone—for every discipline and level of education and for you as an e-tivity designer!

Acknowledgements for this chapter

I asked for help from the fantastic Association of Learning Technology's community and the following people enhanced this chapter. Thank you to Jo Axe, Chara Balasubramaniam, Dawne Bell, Jane Brotchie, Sarah Chesney, Sharon Gardner, Darren Gash, Doug Gowan, Peter Hartley, Oriel Kelly, Emma King, Lesley Pyke, Daniel Scott and Thomas Wanner.

Chapter 5

Deploying e-tivities

A team approach

Part I: About Carpe Diem

One very good way of getting e-tivities designed and deployed for learning and teaching in your organization is to use a team-based learning design process called Carpe Diem, which includes a two-day workshop. The idea behind Carpe Diem was that every moment of the time during the workshop would be spent on designing something that could be put into immediate use with participants—so I used the term '*carpe diem*', the Latin for 'seize the day'. It's a practical response to the essential truth that developing learning with technology cannot be a 'solo' activity but instead a design and 'ecological' experience (Ellis and Goodyear, 2010; Laurillard, 2012).

A Carpe Diem workshop is focused on practical and contextualized outcomes for one particular course, unit, module or programme team. Such workshops complement individual staff and professional development activities, but they are quite different. The promise to those taking part is: 'Get your unit, module, course, programme quickly online—together.'

Roots and branches of Carpe Diem

The Carpe Diem process was created through research and prototyping in 2001, originally at Glasgow Caledonian University in Scotland. I first developed

Carpe Diem workshops when I was a visiting professor at the Caledonian Business School. Feedback from participating staff from the first three workshops (Salmon, 2003), plus feedback from students when the courses were first presented (Siddiqui and Roberts, 2004), indicated that students were engaged and happy with the e-tivities designed during Carpe Diems, and that there was visible confidence building among academics in using the LMS/ VLE for student activities. The team approach resulted in better professional relationships, which were sustained after the intervention.

The Carpe Diem model was stable enough to be tried by others, and for facilitators to be trained. Further testing and transfer with subject teams at the University of Bournemouth and Anglia Ruskin University resulted in increased understanding of, adjustment to and adoption of the model by others such as those at Kingston University (Malone, 2004).

Carpe Diem has since been developed, trialled and scaled-up, especially in the UK, Scandinavia, South Africa and Australia. Although I was the originator and have stayed with Carpe Diem for some 12 years now, it has been worked on by hundreds of people, mainly learning technologists, educationalists, teachers and academics from many disciplines, in the spirit of openness and with the purpose of enabling learners and teachers to benefit from the five-stage model and e-tivities in the best possible ways.

Professor Alejandro Armellini worked with me for some five years at the University of Leicester, where Carpe Diem was extensively deployed in the university and elsewhere. His reflections are on pages 93–4. I have included a much fuller description of the Leicester work in the second part of this chapter (pages 78–84).

Since my move to work in Australia, Carpe Diem has been further developed at the University of Southern Queensland (www.usq.edu.au, see pages 88–91) and at Swinburne University of Technology (www.swinburne. edu.au, see pages 86–8).

Deploying Carpe Diem for e-tivities

See Resources for Practitioners 21, page 186 for a step-by-step process.

But first, let me describe how you can build and deploy e-tivities into new learning designs!

At the heart of this intervention is a two-day workshop in which course teams, in collaboration with subject librarians and learning technologists, design e-tivities for effective e-learning and assessment within their online and blended courses. On the first day, the Carpe Diem team produces a blueprint and storyboard for the course, identifying the purpose and main features of the e-tivities they will design. On the second day, participants turn the prototypes into fully functional e-tivities, which they upload to their institutional LMS/VLE.

Also on the second day, a 'reality checker' (a student or staff member external to the Carpe Diem process) reviews the e-tivities and provides feedback from the participants' perspective. The team uses this feedback to adjust and improve the e-tivities. At the end of the workshop, Carpe Diem teams have a series of reality-checked e-tivities running on their LMS/VLE, a storyboard showing the purpose and location of those e-tivities within the course design, and an action plan.

The Carpe Diem facilitator's main role is to ensure that the workshop deliverables meet the pedagogical challenges identified by the course team, drawing on appropriate input from all participants. The facilitator challenges established notions and offers new perspectives in technology-enhanced learning design and assessment. Carpe Diem differs from traditional staff development approaches insofar as it focuses on the learning design needs specific to a course team taking responsibility for a programme of study. Its outputs can be used by the course team immediately and can inform the development of other course components.

Carpe Diem is not a 'how to use my LMS/VLE' workshop. While participants become more skilled in the use of a range of LMS/VLE features, they do so in the process of addressing a learning design challenge that the technology may help them to resolve. Learning technologists and subject librarians provide additional input and support during the intervention.

We have found that two extra meetings are most helpful: one preparing the Carpe Diem team two to four weeks beforehand and another about two to four weeks after the main workshop. The pre-meeting is an initial contact between the facilitator and the course team for preparation and motivation, and is followed up by a meeting designed to plan for the embedding of the changes into the course. If you have the time and resources, there are some other optional activities that are beneficial (see Resources for Practitioners 23, page 199).

Benefits of trying out the Carpe Diem development process

Experience in running Carpe Diems has shown that the process has quite a few benefits.

- It's a tried and well-rehearsed method using strong, practical, pedagogical principles, focusing e-learning or blended learning on activity, engagement and group work.
- It's an easy way of enabling academics, teachers and educational technologists to design, embed and deliver e-tivities and the five-stage model.
- It introduces, enthuses and offers a pragmatic way of introducing excellent practice in flexible e-learning.
- It changes the minds of many individuals and groups who thought e-learning was difficult and demanding and/or not suitable for their subject: they often go on to encourage others to try it.
- It offers a small investment in time for a specific outcome: the model drives learning design from a pedagogical base, but incorporates learning technologies.
- It achieves successful, productive, collaborative work between academics, tutors, learning designers, librarians and technologists.
- It successfully promotes and deploys the educational organization's LMS/VLE (often underexploited), a digital library if there is one and open educational resources (OERs).
- It reinforces the concept of design once, delivers many times, i.e. a more cost-effective and student-centred way of designing learning than spending many hours 'writing' a course with considerable 'hand-crafting'.

Carpe Diem is suitable for:

- the design of new courses and redesign of existing ones;
- campus, blended and distance modes;
- any level of education or sector;
- any short course, unit, module or programme;
- any discipline;
- any LMS/VLE.

You will need:

- an academic or teaching team willing to commit two full days of their time;
- a module or programme the team needs to design, or an existing one that needs revamping for online or blended learning;
- access to some electronic resources that the team will use for developing an agreed design plan, including learning outcomes, but preferably with

some flexibility around the learning approaches, technology and modes of delivery and assessment;

- 'reality checkers', who will join in for an hour or two at about halfway through day 2 of the workshop;
- a space for the workshop to take place: day 1 needs lots of whiteboards, flip chart paper, pens and coloured sticky notes, or electronic equivalents (plus food and coffee);
- Day 2 needs networked computers—fixed or laptop or a combination, and access to the LMS/VLE (plus food and coffee . . .);
- a Carpe Diem facilitator with good knowledge of the Carpe Diem method and experience in e-tivity design. The facilitator leads the workshop using the Carpe Diem model and process, with pre-prepared activities and resources, to make the most of the team's time together;
- resources to help you from the Carpe Diem section in this book (pages 186–96). There are more on the book's website (www.e-tivities.com).

Inviting teams: key information

- Make it clear that Carpe Diem is not 'staff development', but a supported and developmental team activity.
- Bring in other professions from your organization to work with the subject teams. Carpe Diem teams should include a trained Carpe Diem facilitator with pedagogical knowledge (particularly about e-tivities and the five-stage model), a subject librarian and a learning technologist plus the subject specialists. All course team members and other professionals are expected to be present and participate throughout the two-day workshop, so they need to understand the commitment.
- Choose a new course, or one transferring from a different mode of learning, to incorporate new technologies or approaches.
- The curriculum and learning outcomes should be agreed by the subject group before they arrive in the workshop. Inevitably some discussions on content ensue, but the Carpe Diem facilitator helps prevent content discussions dominating the pedagogical and learning design discussions.
- Only stable 'tried-and-tested' technologies are used so that the focus can shift to pedagogy and the learning experience as soon as possible. Typically these technologies are the LMS/VLE and the digital library, although now a much wider range of technologies are being tried out.
- No computers should be used until a 'blueprint' and a 'storyboard' are agreed upon by the team (see Resources for Practitioners 21, pages 190–3).

Part 2: the University of Leicester's story of the impact of Carpe Diems

In 2005, the University of Leicester launched a strategic initiative to transform its e-learning and distance learning. Leicester's first pedagogical innovation strategy was accepted by its Senate in July 2005. It set up the Beyond Distance Research Alliance to provide evidence and leadership for the changes. The pedagogical innovations introduced and researched under this initiative have built up institutional capacity for evidence-based change, both at Leicester and elsewhere. In particular, they have transformed course design through low-cost, high-value-for-learning approaches. I was deeply involved in this initiative and the Carpe Diem workshops were a key part of the transformation.

For example, in 2008–9 the University of Leicester was awarded the title of University of the Year by *The Times Higher Education*. *The Times Good University Guide 2010* ranked Leicester 15th in England and that followed other rankings in the top 20 for Leicester in the 2008–9 academic year by the *Independent*, *The Sunday Times* and the *Guardian*. In the 2008 (UK) National Student Survey, 92 per cent of full-time students taught at Leicester were satisfied with their programme. This was a level of satisfaction exceeded only by Cambridge among mainstream universities teaching full-time students in England.

The key concept in the University's evolution was that change should be evidence-based. Research generates the evidence: academics can relate to that. They find evidence more convincing than targets, and direct support for transforming learning design better than staff development. They can move from research into practice. With this concept in mind, we set out to create research and development projects and to obtain external funds for them. We saw transformation as happening at four different levels: *individual* > *course team* > *departmental* > *institutional*.

The journey started in a fortunate way: the University had just adopted a new open, forward-looking vision for its teaching and learning. At the same time the UK Higher Education Academy (HEA) had announced that it would support benchmarking of e-learning across several universities.

Benchmarking of e-learning

The first e-learning benchmarking, conducted in early 2006, was a pilot for the subsequent programme, since nothing quite like it had been done before. A great advantage of benchmarking is that you can see how you compare with your partners, as well as seeing which are your strong points and which are weak ones, if any. In this case, Leicester identified—through the benchmarking —'Instructional Design/Pedagogy' and 'Learning Materials' as the key criteria on which it scored lower than others. The second benchmarking, a year after the first, showed success. On a scale of 1 to 6, 'Instructional Design/Pedagogy' had moved up from 2.0 to 4.0, while 'Learning Materials' had gone from 3.0 to 4.0.

We undertook a project that we called ADELIE (Advanced Design for E-learning Institutional Embedding), an HEA-funded Pathfinder project. ADELIE was led by the Beyond Distance Research Alliance, of which I was the Director. Alejandro Armellini led ADELIE, which aimed to develop capacity in learning design throughout the institution. From October 2006, ADELIE fostered incremental change in e-learning design and online teaching practice at Leicester.

ADELIE included extending and developing Carpe Diem as a key part of the change process. Leicester recognized that Carpe Diem promotes and supports change in learning design and assessment, builds institutional capacity and fosters scalable pedagogical innovation (Armellini and Jones, 2008). Carpe Diem workshops were grounded in partnerships that grew between the ADELIE team, learning technologists, subject librarians and academic subject teams. Carpe Diem workshops enabled the teams to understand, develop and implement effective e-learning designs, making use of low-cost, high-impact stable technologies such as the University's LMS/VLE and e-library. Carpe Diems also enabled teams to apply a sustainable 'design once, deliver many times' approach, for the benefit of tutors and learners alike.

ADELIE also included three-week asynchronous e-moderating online courses, based on the five-stage model (Salmon, 2011) and the e-tivities framework. We invited Carpe Diem participants and our academic and support colleagues to take part in these online courses, to transfer the key e-moderating skills (welcoming, encouraging participation, weaving and summarizing) needed to maximize the impact of the new e-tivities during course delivery. As always, we worked on the principle that the better the design of e-tivities, the easier the e-moderation.

The uptake of ADELIE represented a significant success: it generated change across the University. First, 16 course teams from 11 departments, including 87 academics, five subject librarians and five support staff, were involved in Carpe Diem. Of the 16 teams, 12 focused on distance learning (a priority for the University); we also ran four e-moderator courses, involving 38 university teachers from 18 departments.

In addition, we also set up a research dissemination framework we called 'The Media Zoo'. The Zoo concept is based on the four quadrants of Leicester's innovation strategy and is a highly accessible way of communicating evidence and research findings in design and learning transformations.

Born out of ADELIE, CHEETAH (Change by Embedding E-learning in Teaching Across Higher Education Institutions (HEIs)) was a knowledge-transfer and networking project. We developed partnerships with six universities that had been in the Benchmarking and Pathfinder Programme (University of Bath, University College Falmouth, Leeds Metropolitan University, Newman University College, Oxford Brookes University and University of Worcester) to enable them to develop and enhance their institutional capability in e-learning design. We set out to transfer to them from ADELIE our key know-how, models, frameworks and lessons learned about how to support course teams by embedding good practice in e-learning design.

Perhaps not surprisingly, given the earlier success with Carpe Diem, we decided to use the same process again. It was by then a well-researched, well-rehearsed and proven instrument for capacity building in successful learner-centred design. We wanted to facilitate the cascading of the Carpe Diem model to all our partners. We also expected there would be opportunities for additional knowledge transfer, support and dissemination within CHEETAH. We held a Carpe Diem workshop at each of the six partner institutions. Before, during and after each workshop we collected from course teams data that we analysed using Kirkpatrick's four-level evaluation model (Kirkpatrick and Kirkpatrick, 2005): (1) reaction, (2) learning, (3) behaviour and (4) results.

As a very worthwhile extra, we invited colleagues from Oxford Brookes University to run a two-day 'intensive' workshop at Leicester. These 'intensives' share features with Carpe Diem, such as focus, overall aims, target audience and duration, but differ in relation to structure, methodology, pre- and post-workshop activities, resources and deliverables. Both we and our Oxford Brookes colleagues benefited from this exchange: it provided insights into more ways to conduct an effective two-day workshop.

ADELIE showed us that multiple Carpe Diem interventions were needed in an institution if the cascading of the model was to be effective and long-lasting. Would-be facilitators need to attend more than one Carpe Diem where they can watch an experienced Carpe Diem facilitator. Colleagues who went to two or more Carpe Diem workshops had the chance to 'shadow' a more experienced facilitator and lead on some workshop components, and they gained the confidence needed to facilitate customized in-house Carpe Diem sessions.

The process developed local expertise and built institutional capacity, essential for effective cascading and change. All the partners found their CHEETAH experience most valuable and enjoyable, and two said their Carpe Diem was the biggest enabler of the change process. They told us that course teams were willing to commit their time to a researched, tried-and-tested approach. Carpe Diem was vital in securing these teams' participation. They gained new e-learning design skills and had practical exposure to pedagogical benefits of Web 2.0 technologies in course redesign. All the teams designed e-tivities in their institutional LMS/VLE. They now have plans to customize and cascade Carpe Diem internally.

Assessment in learning design: ADDER

Next, the UK HEA granted us funds for ADDER (Assessment and Disciplines: Developing E-tivities Research), which compared and contrasted uses of e-tivities for assessment in three disciplines (Inter-Professional Education in Health, Media Studies and Psychology). We worked with four UK universities (De Montfort University, the University of Derby, London South Bank University and the University of Northampton) over 12 months. In ADDER, we set out to investigate the similarities and differences in assessment practices that make use of e-tivities in those three disciplines, and the impact of these practices on the learner experience.

Carpe Diem was again the key intervention used to generate change in e-learning design and e-tivity-based assessment at all the partner institutions. Seven full Carpe Diem processes were run, during which we observed and recorded what happened. Afterwards, online surveys were used to capture tutors' views of e-tivities and assessment. We also conducted interviews with six tutors and constructed from these cognitive maps (Eden, 2004). The course teams designed e-tivities during and after the workshops; they also wrote module handbooks and programme specifications, and we had access to these resources.

The typology accommodated uses of e-tivities for assessment that had not been identified in ADELIE (Armellini, Jones and Salmon, 2007). There was significant use of collaborative Web 2.0 technologies to enhance learner interaction and collaboration (Armellini and Jones, 2008), which took pressure off the tutors and involved students as feedback providers. ADDER enabled cascading of Carpe Diem within and across the ADDER partner institutions as well as informing the assessment approaches for future Carpe Diems.

New technologies in learning design: DUCKLING

The journey continued! The Joint Information Systems Committee (JISC)-funded DUCKLING project (Delivering University Curricula: Knowledge, Learning and Innovation Gains) began in November 2008 and ran for two years. It developed advanced delivery, presentation and assessment processes to enhance the work-based learning experience of students studying remotely. DUCKLING demonstrated the practical marriage of sound approaches to deploying new technologies and work-based pedagogy for learning support, communication and assessment for professional adult learners. Amongst the DUCKLING objectives were enhancing learner-centred curriculum delivery deploying the LMS/VLE and well-established peer and collaborative e-tivities. The outcomes were some major transformations of work-based student learning opportunities, plus evidence for sustainable embedding of innovations. DUCKLING capitalized on the affordances of three technologies (podcasting, e-book readers and 3-D virtual worlds) to enhance the university's delivery of two distance learning MA programmes in Occupational Psychology and one in the School of Education in Applied Linguistics, and Teaching English to Speakers of Other Languages (TESOL).

All three programmes faced similar challenges: the need to improve the quantity and quality of interactions between students and tutors, the quality of the course materials (perceived as 'too dry' by learners), personalization and the provision of added mobility and flexibility. Specific pedagogical challenges in Psychology revolved around assessment, including dissertation and essay support and guidance, supervision, research methods and feedback. In Education, the focus was on using each medium for what it does best for learning and teaching: for example, audio for varieties of spoken English and discourse analysis.

The course teams had already undertaken Carpe Diem workshops, so for DUCKLING we created a shorter intervention to enable them to design and produce effective podcasts and integrate them into their courses. These went live almost immediately. Podcasting became embedded in the courses through development in Carpe Diem workshops and made a very significant difference to the quality of the learner experience.

Open educational resources: OTTER

During our journey, the Beyond Distance Research Alliance and its partners covered more and more ground. The HEA and UK JISC-funded Open,

Transferable and Technology-enabled Educational Resources (OTTER) project set out to pilot and evaluate systems and processes designed to enable individuals, teams and departments to release high-quality open educational resources (OERs) for free access, reuse and repurposing by others, in perpetuity. OTTER contributed a body of high-quality OERs from nine departments at Leicester. These OERs are free to access online, use, adapt and repurpose under an appropriate open licence, and are valuable to academics, past, current and future learners, funding agencies and professional organizations in the relevant fields worldwide. OTTER makes extensive use of learning technologies and maximized the affordances of the JorumOpen platform and Leicester's institutional open source platform, Plone. OTTER has informed institutional and sector policy on the release of existing digital content as OERs.

OERs have played a significant role in Carpe Diem since 2006. Course teams have integrated materials from a range of sources, especially as sparks, which have improved course design and very significantly reduced the amount of time, cost and effort required for development and production. OTTER and its JISC-funded sister projects offer a set of additional resources for enhanced learning design, all readily available for immediate use, repurposing and reuse. OTTER OERs continue to offer a significant low-cost, high-value resource for all future Carpe Diems for Leicester and any organization using the model.

Summarizing the lessons

Strategic transformation using the Carpe Diem model has happened at all four levels: individual, course team, departmental and institutional. We know that individuals are responsible for changing their own practice and welcoming these changes. However, it is also clear that 'one academic doesn't make a transformation'; neither do many academics if they are in isolated situations in a wide variety of departments, schools or faculties. Therefore, we continue to encourage and maximize individual contacts to lead towards Carpe Diem workshops and teamwork wherever achievable.

There are positive feedback loops from the spark of interest from individual or small groups of academics, to the Carpe Diem facilitator to Carpe Diem workshops and back again. One course team undertaking a Carpe Diem frequently results in others requesting support in departmental workshops in e-learning.

The University of Leicester Learning Innovation Strategy ran from 2009 to 2012. The principles on which the strategy is based are largely derived from the Carpe Diem experiences and evidence for change. They include evidence for and evaluation of benefits of enabling innovation across the institution for students' learning; collaboration across the institution within strategic frameworks and through funded research and development projects; raising the capability of all members of the University—students and staff—to exploit and benefit from the learning technologies; and exploring 'beyond the obvious' to prepare for the future in unseen, unknown and uncharted territory for learning and teaching. We now recognize the complex links, communication pathways and lines of influence from individuals to institutional capacity and the need to ensure a cascading and enhanced process of dissemination to build towards positive and successful transformation of the experience of all Leicester's learners.

Stories from the front line 5

Catriona Burke at the Kemmy Business School, University of Limerick, Ireland, tells us about her colleagues' experiences of redesigning a Masters programme through Carpe Diems.

Our Centre for Project Management (CPM) in the Kemmy Business School at the University of Limerick specializes in Masters programmes in project management. We offered our programme by distance learning from 1999 to 2011, for post-experience, part-time learners in full-time employment. This version was print-based and content heavy; a network of local tutors provided support across four centres within Ireland.

We wanted to give our dispersed students greater flexibility and to extend our reach beyond Ireland. We took the opportunity to develop a new model of learning emphasizing interaction, dialogue and collaboration—and to leave the 'transmission' mode of teaching behind us. Our students have significant industry experience; we wanted to use that experience to promote an informed process of interaction between what is known and what is to be learned. We hoped to encourage our students to be independent thinkers with their own emerging theories of the world. We planned to create a sense of community and peer support within the group. We wanted our teachers to become facilitators and guides rather than 'sages on the stage'. We had the Moodle LMS/VLE available to us.

Learning design

During a visit to the University of Leicester in early 2011, we realized that Carpe Diem outcomes could include the kind of learning environment we wanted to create for our students. We began two-day Carpe Diem workshops in March 2011. We held three to enable us to redesign the first six modules for Year 1 of our Masters of Science (MSc) in Project and Programme Management. The core team of the Centre and programme directors, a learning technologist and our faculty librarian attended all of the Carpe Diems. Academics assigned to each individual module attended one Carpe Diem each.

Stage 1 of the first Carpe Diem, the section 'Writing a Blueprint', triggered a detailed discussion around our teaching philosophy and a shift away from content-heavy modules to much more interactivity. After our Carpe Diem facilitator explained how e-tivities add value to the learning, it became clear to us that e-tivities would enable us to apply our newly agreed philosophy: they are now at the core of our model.

We found the Carpe Diem process to be a very practical and outcomes-based intervention and enormously helpful in developing the team's ability to undertake new learning design, particularly e-tivities. By the end of each Carpe Diem, each course team had a set of e-tivities, a blueprint for each module, a storyboard and a practical action plan.

The workshops were followed up with support to staff. We provided an area on the Moodle LMS/VLE dedicated to supporting academics teaching in online environments. It included a wide variety of skills development, including how to create podcasts and how to make links. We continued to answer queries and reality-check of new e-tivities.

Nine months after the initial visit to Leicester, we began teaching the first students. The MSc is now based on three modules per semester, run sequentially, each with a typical duration of five weeks. At the start of each module, students are presented with a learning pathway that makes explicit links between module learning outcomes, materials and sparks, e-tivities and assessment. Students are clear from the outset how meaningful engagement with e-tivities will contribute to their ability to complete successfully each module. Students are typically required to complete one to two e-tivities per week and some modules offer marks for these.

We decided to focus on e-tivities that would require individual postings to discussion forums and Wikis in the initial weeks of the programme, later extending to audio-based and group-based e-tivities in order to scaffold students' engagement through the five-stage model.

Outcomes

The initial cohort of 24 students posted in excess of 17,000 words across two separate e-tivities in the first week of the MSc. They were engaged! The first cohort are achieving very well, with an average grade point in line with what is expected at a Masters' level within the University.

Our new design has enabled us to market to learners further afield. We are now supporting students across nine different countries. We expect to continue to expand our market reach.

The Carpe Diems enabled us to achieve our goals for change and transition to a new model of learning design and delivery. Carpe Diems proved an excellent forum for fostering innovation. We have grown in confidence, not just in designing e-tivities but also in delivery and e-moderation. We have started to showcase the evidence of success of the new programme across our institution. We hope that others may find that Carpe Diems and introducing e-tivities will help them to achieve their goals too. Carpe Diems have given our staff new competence in e-learning design and delivery.

Stories from the front line 6

Sharmini Thurairasa, a convenor and lecturer at Swinburne University of Technology in Melbourne, Australia, tells us about her use of Carpe Diem for the redesign of a campus-based course for blended delivery.

I am the principal convenor for, and teach, Social Networking in Organizations to on-campus undergraduate students in Years 1–3. The units had been delivered for two semesters on campus. I was looking for a way of engaging students of the i-generation who regularly use new technologies to learn for themselves.

I was introduced to Carpe Diems and the five-stage model in a series of talks given by Professor Gilly Salmon. I signed up for a Carpe Diem workshop, because I wanted to try different ways of engaging students and keeping their attention as well as being able to test their knowledge of the educational material. Having read about how social networking tools have changed how formal learning takes place, I decided to re-invent, with help from Gilly and her colleagues, a unit I was teaching that seemed to lend itself to a blended mode.

I knew I had to have a team of people with different skills to help me with this change. I solicited help from three: Cathy Pocknee, a learning designer; Kim Hodgman, the academic liaison librarian and support person; and Catherine Lang, a subject specialist teaching this unit. I took on two roles: as second subject specialist and as technical designer.

We had a month in which to design and prepare the unit before going live! The whole team undertook a full Carpe Diem workshop over two days as soon as we could. We examined on day 1 the learning objectives, material and assessments that we've used in the past. It was a very intensive schedule that resulted in a revamped unit. Brainstorming enabled us to come up with new 'sparks' but maintain the knowledge acquisition that we expected of students. On day 2 we managed to get in three 'reality checkers' who gave us some tips for improvement in sample e-tivities created by the team during the workshop. We created deliverables: a storyboard, four e-tivities and an action plan for further e-tivity development. We brainstormed ideas, learned from each other and helped with the unit's change of delivery from a weekly face-to-face one-hour laboratory, one-hour tutorial and one-hour lecture to blended learning using e-tivities plus on- and offline guest speakers.

After the Carpe Diem, we produced a further 22 e-tivities in a month before the semester began. I developed each e-tivity, then shared it with Catherine L., who provided feedback on any changes required. Once these were done we sent the e-tivity to Cathy P. and Kim to look at learning design and copyright as well as for further comments. After final changes, the e-tivities were released onto the Blackboard LMS. When the semester started, we were ready—having completed the process for 15 e-tivities!

During the semester we met the students for a weekly one-hour lecture but designed readings and e-tivities to fill the allocated laboratory and tutorial hours. We introduced several 'getting-to-know-you' e-tivities before the first lecture. I co-ordinated class lists and ensured our LMS site was open two weeks before the semester, so that we could publish announcements and explain what students needed to do before we met them. I used the first lecture to talk about what we had learned about them and thus got through Access and Motivation, Stage 1 of the five-stage model.

We led students into Stage 2 (Socialization) with highly interactive e-tivities. We team members visited the website often too: this was received quite well by students who had enrolled at the beginning, but it was difficult for late enrollers to benefit. By week 4 of the semester, we had introduced e-tivities that involved more teamwork to get them further into Stages 3 and 4 (Information Exchange and Knowledge Construction). In week 5 we gave them a multiple-choice test to assess their information exchange and readings they had discussed in class and online.

The e-tivities continued all through the semester, including some related to the guest speakers, to promote knowledge construction. In week 9 we gave them a multiple-choice test with a case study. Their final assessment was based on students' work in small teams: they had to create and agree on an idea, develop a mock website including the use of social networking tools and applications, and present to each other and us on the process they had followed.

A technical problem was implementing all this within our Blackboard LMS environment. We could not introduce timed releases well, so there were problems in opening and closing e-tivities throughout the semester. Although we explained in our first lecture (face-to-face) what students had to do for each e-tivity (i.e. first answering the question in the e-tivity and coming back several days later to respond to others), some participants did not fully grasp this. Also, I found that giving feedback was time-consuming until I had more experience of e-moderating.

I enjoyed the Carpe Diem and rolling out the unit in its new form. It enabled me to discover a much easier and engaging way of building curriculum into units. For example, we can slot different material and e-tivities into the unit and pull things out that do not go so well, without losing the knowledge content. I am planning to implement this approach in another unit I teach.

Some students were teaching us how they used the technology and what worked for them and what did not, so we are making changes to some e-tivities for next semester. I am trying to implement a better learning activity management system integrated within Blackboard. This will help us to include timed delivery, close off past e-tivities as we move through the semester, send reminders to students and deliver material more effectively than we did in this past semester.

Stories from the front line 7

Dr Shirley Reushle is a Carpe Diem facilitator at the University of Southern Queensland (USQ), Australia, and Associate Professor Jill Lawrence is a course leader in the Faculty of Arts. They talk about their experience of the Carpe Diem process, how the students received the redesigned course and the impact it has had on learning outcomes.

We used the Carpe Diem process to redesign CMS1008 Building Professional Nursing Attributes A. This course is offered each year to 400 students in semester 1 and 150 students in semester 2. Its primary objective is to develop students' literacies and skills they need to succeed as learners in their higher education studies and as nursing professionals. The course had been offered on campus. For 2012, the course was moved online.

The Carpe Diem process was selected because it provides a structured framework for course teams to understand, design, develop and implement e-learning designs. It provided our team with ways of exploring a variety of e-resources and low-cost, high-impact technologies, with practical support to deliver the course in USQ's LMS/VLE Moodle. The team understood that the Carpe Diem was not a technical workshop on how to use Moodle; Carpe Diem participants became more skilled in the use of Moodle features, but they did so while addressing a pedagogical design challenge that the technology might help them to resolve. A learning technologist, librarian and others provided input and support during the Carpe Diem.

The Carpe Diem workshops

We followed the recommended steps: we had a pre-Carpe Diem preparation and information session held by the facilitator with the course team, a two-day facilitated Carpe Diem workshop and a post-Carpe Diem review session. During the workshop, Shirley led the course team through collaborative tasks including blueprinting, storyboarding, team-working, scaffolding of networked learning using the five-stage model, development of e-tivities, peer reviewing, aligned assessment and a follow-up action plan.

Once we had established the mission for the course, the team discussed and agreed the learning outcomes or objectives, which were that learners should be able to:

- identify, integrate and enhance the skills, attributes and competencies they bring with them to university;
- demonstrate and reflect on the skills and literacies essential to ongoing professional practice;
- read and write critically in their study and professional contexts;
- apply an understanding of graduate qualities in building their personal and professional identity.

Next, we went through a brainstorm to determine topics related to each of the course objectives. Once the topics for the e-tivities were planned, the course team divided into smaller groups to map out the e-tivities, including the sparks, purpose, tasks, instructions, responses and links to feedback.

The next step involved participation by peers to provide feedback about the proposed e-tivities. These 'reality checkers' gave helpful feedback, ensuring the e-tivities, posts and links to assessments were student-centred, engaging and appropriate to the students' anticipated abilities.

The reality checkers continued to assist the design process later as we sought their feedback on several iterations of course design. They gave us feedback on the LMS components, such as our use of Web pages, forum posts and sparks.

For us, Carpe Diem assisted the design process in many ways. For example, the storyboard components helped shift the focus away from the course content and towards students' learning outcomes. E-tivities were scaffolded using the five-stage model and closely aligned to assessment. Students' forum posts, embedded as formative assessment in the e-tivities and in the formal assessment, ensured that student feedback and opinion were integral parts of course design. The reflective components of the assessment also contributed feedback about the online processes involved.

Carpe Diem had a positive impact on how the course team viewed the course design process and the course itself. It provided an efficient and effective way to incorporate an online pedagogy into what had previously been an on-campus course.

Our students concurred:

> For me technological engagement in the course has made my dream to study nursing a reality and has removed any concern I had about feeling isolated as a distance learner. JS

> My online digital and literacy skills this semester have definitely been developed while working through CMS1008. The weekly online study materials including sparks, PowerPoints, lectures, e-tivities, forum posts, and introduction to Wiki links have meant that I maintain regular and up-to-date, online engagement. VL

Student feedback indicated that students who said they had bypassed the e-tivities either failed or only just passed the assessment:

> When it came time for the assignment I thought I would be fine. I did not think that missing a few postings would be a big deal. I was very wrong. For the tasks I had done the forum postings for, I did not have an issue then as I got further on and deeper into the assignment I found it harder and harder. I regretted not doing the tasks. EM

The e-tivities also gave students the confidence to engage online:

> At first forums took me out of my comfort zone. Since it was a requirement to participate on CMS1008 weekly forums I was eased into making regular contributions as well as reading those of others. I soon became used to it and also found a lot of information that was very helpful and still do. KN

CMS 1008 has also helped me in the use of online forums. I wouldn't have written on the online forums if it weren't for e-tivities to prod me along. I would probably have felt a little bit worried I'd write something incorrect or silly, but . . . has given me the confidence to write on the appropriate forums regarding class matters. DH

The Carpe Diem process provided the course leaders with a very do-able process to convert an on-campus course to a fully online course with inbuilt peer support in a number of areas: ICT and the LMS, the library, the first-year experience. The course was conducted again in semester 2, bearing in mind the feedback from peers and students. Our changes were mostly about reorganizing the LMS structure a bit. We are now applying the Carpe Diem process to other courses that we teach.

Stories from the front line 8

A group of colleagues got together to attempt to solve a specific problem through deploying Carpe Diem design principles. Carpe Diem facilitator Simon Kear takes up the story.

A UK-based organization under the National Institute for Health Research, called Collaboration for Leadership in Applied Health Research and Care (CLAHRC-LNR) and covering three English counties, had a specific long-term challenge to address. It sought to overcome the barriers to implementing research into health care provision. It brought together the local health organizations in partnership with the University of Leicester as part of a five-year programme to ensure that the lessons learned from research studies are rapidly and effectively put into practice.

CLAHRC-LNR was investigating how it could offer an alternative to managing and hosting face-to-face workshops. It works with all kinds of health staff—nurses, doctors, consultants and carers—and it was becoming increasingly difficult to find a time when busy staff could attend. The workshops were expensive to run and their effectiveness for staff that attended was felt to be minimal. We were asked to help run a Carpe Diem to provide an online design.

Two Carpe Diem facilitators worked in August 2011 with a small CLAHRC-LNR team of five, which consisted of the training co-ordinators and teaching staff. The Carpe Diem workshop followed the six key stages in Carpe Diem. We started by discussing, identifying and agreeing on a mission statement, the intended audience and the learning outcomes for the course. We agreed that there was to be no formal assessment but participants would receive a certificate of completion.

This first part was invaluable in creating a forum for the course team to talk to each other with only a little guidance from the facilitators. A clear idea of what the course was about and what it needed to achieve quickly emerged. The traditional teaching staff expressed scepticism about moving the learning into the online environment, but this soon dissipated as we began to create the storyboard and the e-tivity designs.

On the second day the course team enthusiastically built prototypes of their e-tivities. They included technologies such as wikis, discussion forums, audio podcasts and narrated slideshows.

The result was a pilot two-week online course called Implementing Evidence in Clinical Practice, which was hosted on a LMS/VLE Moodle platform. The course contains four e-tivities. It requires around eight hours of study time. The output from the final e-tivity is a bespoke printable plan for implementing clinical evidence, a plan that professionals can apply in their everyday roles. Course participants also receive a completion certificate that they can add to their continuous professional development (CPD) portfolio.

Feedback from the first eight participants on this pilot course was positive. One complaint was the 'clunkiness' of the wiki in the version of Moodle in use. We decided to keep the wiki but to include a comprehensive guide for using it. We knew from the start that the course participants were very time-poor so we were unsurprised when they felt they needed more time to complete the e-tivities. We decided not to remove any e-tivities but to emphasize the time commitments that would be required of participants before they signed up to take part.

Outcomes

Moving online provided a flexible answer to a significant problem for CLAHRC-LNR. CLAHRC-LNR needed a solution that was lower-cost but also engaging, practical, scalable and sustainable. The use of an LMS/VLE and the development of good e-tivities offered this. Carpe Diem provided a quick way to help the course team to understand what was required and to develop a usable design.

The feedback from course participants showed that the learning outcomes had been achieved, giving participants the skills and a working plan for applying recent research findings in their everyday clinical practice.

CLAHRC-LNR will run their own internal Carpe Diem workshops to produce two more online courses to be made available in 2013.

Stories from the front line 9

Alejandro Armellini is Professor of Learning and Teaching in Higher Education at the University of Northampton in the UK. He has been working with Carpe Diem and e-tivities for some six years and reflects on his practice.

I chose the Carpe Diem workshop model to bring together course teams and offer them a common focus in collaboratively designing an effective and engaging course. I found that sometimes team members met for the first time during the Carpe Diem workshop! From my experience, Carpe Diems are successful because they enable course teams to design for task-based, student-centred online or blended learning.

I use e-tivities because they enable the team to design with student participation for learning as a focus—rather than delivery of content. E-tivities are powerful tools: at the design stage, academics and teachers visualize and generate the scaffold needed for learning outcomes to align with assessment. During delivery, e-tivities help learners to engage meaningfully and actively with course materials and processes, both individually and in groups. Learners also use e-tivities to provide evidence of their development towards the achievement of their learning outcomes.

I encourage others to use e-tivities because one of their key features is simplicity: they are simple and quick to design, comfortable to engage with, uncomplicated to manage and e-moderate, and flexible enough to be adapted and reused with a variety of technologies. They enhance learning experiences and save time.

I have found that the storyboard element of Carpe Diem is central to understanding the usefulness of the five-stage model: the team can map out assessments, e-tivities and content (in that order!) to ensure alignment, provide a scaffolded development pathway, and maximize learner motivation and effectiveness of group work. Over the years, I have facilitated and researched more than 70 Carpe Diems and supported course teams as they have moved from planning to development, piloting, delivery and evaluation. Good facilitation of Carpe Diem is the key to success. The facilitator needs to be credible, innovative and an evidence-based problem solver—able to see pedagogical problems and a range of solutions from the perspective of the course team members and their students.

Through my practice, I have introduced innovation into Carpe Diem and e-tivity design. I have refined, improved and disseminated the process over time and enabled other colleagues to run it, including more extensive approaches to storyboarding (see page 191), resource audits (see page 200) and expanding the work on e-tivities that can be done online by the team prior to, during and after the two-day workshop, which I call 'layering'.

My next plans include developing the University of Northampton's Learning and Teaching Plan, to focus on the enhancement of the quality of learning and teaching and developing capability across all six schools. As part of my new role, I am spreading Carpe Diem (called 'CAIeRO' at Northampton) and e-tivities across the University. The plan involves:

- running exemplar Carpe Diems, with apprentice Carpe Diem facilitators, to enable us to disseminate and share good practice in facilitating workshops and offering Carpe Diems more extensively;
- observing and providing feedback on Carpe Diems facilitated by the Learning and Teaching Co-ordinators based at each of the six schools at Northampton, with support from the Learning Technology team;
- encouraging, and in future perhaps mandating, Carpe Diems as an integral component of the programme validation and re-validation processes.

I have drawn very heavily in the second part of this chapter from Armellini, Salmon and Hawkridge, 2009, Chapter 10. Many thanks to my co-authors, Professors David Hawkridge and Alejandro Armellini, the book editors and the UK Higher Education Academy for permission.

Part 2:

RESOURCES FOR PRACTITIONERS

IDEAS

Resources for practitioners 1

Ideas for
e-tivities

Many of these ideas for e-tivities can be used at several stages of the five-stage model. The key issue is how deeply you expect the participants to go in their responses, how much time you allow them and the e-moderator's skills at weaving and summarizing. So the level at which I've placed them is indicative only. Experiment and look carefully at outcomes!

All the ideas will work within discussion forums, social media or any platform that is interactive and participative. Most will work just as well if participants are accessing them on the move and/or from mobile devices.

Many of my examples are from business or education because I am more familiar with these disciplines. However, I am sure you will be able to see how to substitute sparks and processes from your own topics, contexts, disciplines or organizations.

Whatever you use, try the e-tivity invitational frameworks (see pages 2–3), and be clear about your purpose (see page 38).

Stage 1: Access and motivation

At this stage offer easy e-tivities that are quickly achieved while giving practice in the use of the technology. E-moderators might sometimes have to offer a little one-to-one help and acknowledgement to ensure positive attitudes towards the start of the experience.

If you are planning to assess the experience, process or journey of online learning as well as the outcomes, encourage regular 'point of learning' individual or group reflections from Stage 1 onwards. Participants may not see the value of them at this point so will need fairly structured opportunities to reflect. However, they will set up a good spark for later use.

If you are feeling adventurous, try adding a social media platform or two from Stage 1 onwards (see Chapter 4).

Icebreakers

Each of these will take around two to three weeks online. They are easy to set up and run and will enable your participants to get to know each other, to contribute rather than 'lurk', and to become more familiar with the platform in use in a fairly safe and fun way. Participants can be encouraged to find others with similar interests to share ideas with online, as well as to find learning partners who have different kinds of ideas and support to offer. With sharing and support, more serious topics and discussions go well.

Quiz

Ask each participant to put up a maximum of one screenful of text that reveals a little about them. Offer them a possible structure, such as the choice of three or four from job, home location, personal interests, family, what they hope to get out of the course, what they hope to put in, something they're good at and something they need to get better at. They could offer their learning styles or best contributions to team roles, if they know them. When every participant has contributed, set up a little quiz, based on the group, with a prize—for example, Who has twin girls? Who has a spaniel dog? Who lives in X area? Who works in company Y as a product manager? Publicize the quiz and offer a prize (a useful mobile app?) for the most accurate response or the fastest, or both.

Images

Ask each participant to post a URL into the conference that tells the group's members something about themselves. Put one up about yourself. Triggers might be a hobby, a personal website, Facebook or LinkedIn site, an organizational or corporate site, a picture of a favourite beach, rock band, a country, a book, and so on. Ask each person to post a message saying why they have chosen to share their particular URL with other participants. Run this e-tivity for a week or so only and then archive it.

You could set up a Flickr stream or similar site for everyone's links and pictures. Or try a visual 'recommendations' site such as Pinterest.

If you really want something visual, look up software that offers opportunities for 'self-portraits'.

Organize participants into pairs and get them to combine their images in a new way.

Run a fun e-tivity showing how images can reflect everyday life, or life can reflect art—use sparks from your subject.

My brand

Ask the participants to mention a brand that illustrates something that they always use and say what it says about them. Start a discussion on these brands.

Hall of mirrors

Explain how Web or Facebook sites of organizations often present a more up-to-date image of them than their annual reports, brochures or other print-based publications do. Post five sites and call it 'The Hall of Mirrors'. Ask participants to take a wander round them and post a message saying one or two of the following:

- What are the similarities between the sites?
- Which one would encourage them to buy online and why?
- Which one would put them off buying the product or service and why?
- Which one made them feel confident and which one made them feel nervous?
- What is the brand's footprint in social media such as blogs?
- Does this brand use other social media to present itself?

Think of further questions. Allow participants, say, one week to respond, and then run a discussion on the similarities and differences in responses.

Talents

'Give' each participant a fantasy $200/$1,000/$100,000 to 'spend' online. Allow them one week to wander around the Web and say in a message what they would buy with this sum (and why). If you want to make it course-related, they can investigate products that are relevant to your topic, such as online courses for educators, images for art students, and so on. Start a discussion on the different choices. Has anyone chosen to make money with their $200 rather than spend it? Who has spent it on themselves and who on others? Who has bought goods and who purchased a service?

Wanderlust

Post a URL, Google Map or Street View showing a great location in your home country (for holidays or business). Ask each participant to find and post another great location. Get each person to say what they would do or purchase on a visit to this country. Start a discussion on country specialities and global brands.

Descriptions

Ask participants to describe their study area or perhaps the view from the window. These are much more 'telling' and people often find this activity more comfortable than filling in a profile or saying something 'interesting' about themselves.

Mapping

Using visual mapping software of many kinds is very productive for learning and sharing online. Explore ideas of borders and boundaries and crossing them.

Introduce the power of diagrams for simple ideas at this stage—it'll stand them in great stead throughout the programme and for when concepts become more complex, interactive and adaptive (see example on page 142).

Try crossing other boundaries and disciplines, e.g. the impact of art on science. Do you get the idea? Here are some more:

More suggestions

- Explore the nature of success on the course.
- Each participant offers a contribution to the 'netiquette' of the group. Build a commonly agreed list of the contributions.
- Ask participants to look out of a window and relate a topic—say, critical path analysis, or leadership styles, or decision making—to natural objects such as trees or human-made objects such as traffic furniture. Go with the flow. This works!

- Offer a learning styles or team roles inventory (watch you don't infringe anyone's copyright). Ask participants to discuss their styles and how they think their styles will manifest themselves in the online environment.
- Ask participants what single thing would improve the quality of their online communication. Who could help to achieve this?
- Set up a 'skills and knowledge' market. Each participant states the help that he or she would like from one other participant. In return, they agree to help one other person.
- Set up a 'discovery' area for participants to publish their own tips and tricks on the technology. But edit it so it does not become a 'whinge' area!
- Offer key ideas (we call them 'footprints') developed by previous participants in the course. Ask new arrivals to explore the ideas.
- What would you do with one million ping-pong balls? (A good practice question on Twitter.)
- What is ecotourism?
- How can we describe perfumes and smells online?
- Ask each participant to acknowledge, congratulate or celebrate the contribution of one other participant.
- Ask participants to offer tips for 'surviving online learning'.
- Ask participants to say what they would be doing now if they weren't working online.
- Ask pairs to interview each other by Skype and introduce each other to the group.
- Ask each person to name a famous person from their locality (town, country) and tell us one significant piece of information about this person. Is the information on Wikipedia accurate, or are they mentioned at all? If not, there's an opportunity.
- What's the main method of public transport in your town or city? Why has it dominated?
- Ask participants to mention when they first received a computer on their desk or in their home, and the circumstances. When did they first hear the terms 'superhighway' or 'World Wide Web' and from whom?
- As children, what were your participants' favourite games or toys? Set them up in groups to invent one for a 21st-century digital child.

Continuity and change

As you design Stage 1 and 2 e-tivities, it's good to start with the end in mind.

If you are using Carpe Diem (see Chapter 5), such planning will naturally occur during your storyboarding. But even if you're designing without the full Carpe Diem process, try putting your learning outcomes and assessments in first, then plan your e-tivities sequencing.

Do insist that participants make a note of what they hope, plan and expect to acquire and achieve by taking part and critically what they believe they can offer to others. Remind them to revisit at various points.

Many good Stage 5 e-tivities can be set up at Stage 1 and developed throughout the course. For example, ask participants to establish their under-standings and share them at the very beginning, record them simply in an e-portfolio or personal space tool and then revisit them, and share key insights at this stage. Offer them simple personal development tools to help (there are many online; search for MindTools™, for example).

Stage 2: Socialization

E-tivities at this stage are about getting to know each other, establishing a group to work with and understanding the approach that the group or community will take. Try to use humour, but watch for issues of equality that might arise from it.

There are two main kinds of e-tivity: those that are about getting to know each other and those that clearly look to the learning work that is to come. Many participants will feel impatient with the first type, so such e-tivities may need to be disguised a little. For example, one of the most successful e-tivities I have run with a very varied multicultural group was to ask about their favourite dish of food and why it was important to them. The discussion ran for several weeks and ranged from traditions of meals to cultural festivals. The group bonded in a rare and productive way.

Try to use innovative ways to enable participants to get to know about each other and to be able to form effective learning teams. You may think that some of these suggestions are too lightweight for adult groups. However, one or two of them, carefully chosen, will help establish the group and lead to more in-depth knowledge sharing and learning later on. The following suggestions all work:

- Introduce yourself using six descriptive words.
- What are the most popular given names in your culture? Ask each person to explain the origin of his or her name, the reason it was chosen and any special cultural significance.
- If you were an animal, what would you be? Can we make up a farmyard, zoo, circus or jungle? Create a little free video?
- What musical instruments do you play? Can we form a band or orchestra with our skills and experience? There are mobile apps . . .

- Do you have any domestic pets? Why did you choose this kind of animal? What would happen if our pets met each other? How did you choose their names?
- If we were setting up a business, what could you contribute? What products would you like to make or what processes would you like to set up?
- Offer one website or blog that illustrates your favourite hobby.
- If you were leaving to go on holiday or a business trip, what three essential items would you put in your suitcase? What kind of packer are you? Do you throw everything in and sit on the case? Do you have one or two specially selected items, carefully folded . . . or what? Compare the similarities and differences.
- What's your favourite smell? Can you describe it online? Why is it important to you?
- What's the most important lesson life has taught you/working in this company/living in this place/up until now? For example, starting this education programme.
- Do you play online games? What have you learned about working in groups from them?
- How do you relax?
- Offer a cartoon or humourous picture. Ask for reactions.
- In what circumstances do you behave 'safely' and when might you take 'risks'? Can we find common categories?
- What's your favourite town? Take us on a virtual tour of it. Each participant comments on whether they have visited for real or virtually.
- What's your favourite journey? Take us along it. Use Google Maps or Street View. Start a discussion based on some feature you see along the way.
- What's the plot of your favourite novel? (Try this with Twitter or other micro-blogging platforms with restricted words or characters.) Compare and contrast the different plots.
- What items would you put in your virtual shopping basket and why? Are there similarities and differences in the group?
- What's your favourite word/expression and why? Can we build them into a story? If you're brave, try Twitter stories.
- If we were to have a fancy dress party, what theme would you choose for this group? What would you come as? What periods of history/literature/ continents of the world would we represent?
- Who's your favourite actor and why? Have we all chosen different people?

- Who's the person you'd most like to meet from your discipline and why? What would he or she say about working online?
- Who's the historical figure you most identify with and why? Would they like the Internet? How would they use it?
- If you were offered a soapbox, what would you talk about? Could you condense the points into 50 words (or whatever the number of characters your micro-blogging software offers)?
- What's your favourite gadget and why? Will it help you communicate on this course?
- What would you like to see invented and why? Are you sure it's not already on YouTube?
- What traditional performing art forms are there in your culture (Brits can try explaining the traditional Winter pantomime to people who have never seen one!).
- What was your proudest moment? ('Most embarrassing moment' could be hilarious . . . but risky!)
- If I ruled the world . . .

Senses

Try to tap into issues that explore similarities and differences across cultures, learning and upbringing. Try also to include at least one e-tivity that taps into senses other than those involved in typing, posting and uploading and reading. We have found the following especially powerful:

- My favourite music. Explore sources and roots of different kinds. Offer websites, iTunes U or YouTube links so participants can listen and exchange ideas.
- My favourite food. If you could live on one dish only, what would it be? What key food do you remember from your childhood? What special dishes are made in your hometown?
- Online wine tasting. Each participant has a glass by his or her keyboard. They describe and discuss the taste, and the origin of the wine.
- What's the best excuse you've heard for the late submission of a piece of work that is to be assessed?
- If we were designing a physical classroom for our group, what features would be important? Where would it be located in the world and why?
- Highlight a topical issue that is relevant to your course. Ask participants to take positions as stakeholders.

● Share silly extrapolations. For example, 'The number of Elvis Presley impersonators has reached an all-time record high—there are now at least 85,000 Elvises around the world, compared to only 170 in 1977 when he died. At this rate of growth, experts predict that by 2019 Elvis impersonators will make up a third of the world's population.' Are the 'facts' correct? Does anyone really think this will happen?

Cross cultures

If you have a wide variety of participants located all over the world, then you have special opportunities for exploring many aspects of diverse cultures and of globalization. You may be able to introduce these as socialization exercises at Stage 2 and carry the themes and outcomes through to Stages 3 and 4.

● Where is your nearest branch of Starbucks or McDonald's? What kinds of buildings or streets are around it? Show us on Google Street View. What conclusions can be drawn?
● Do you drive on the left or right? Why? Should it be changed?
● What are the problems and benefits of the transport systems in your country? What is the preferred mode of transport? How is it funded?
● Does your country have a national dress or costume? Have you ever worn it and when?
● Everyone contribute the words 'please' and 'thank you' or 'hello' and 'goodbye' in their mother languages. Use voice boards and say them. Build a list and try using them out of politeness during the course.

Scenarios

Try offering little scenarios for discussion. These can prepare groups for more demanding case studies at Stage 4. For example:

● You return from a vacation. Your car is parked in the street surrounded by policemen. What has happened?
● You are responsible for marking examination papers for this course. You notice that one candidate appears to have produced answers to completely different questions to those that were set. What might have happened here?
● You have lived in the same apartment for 10 years. It's very quiet. Suddenly the building starts to make a noise at night. What might be happening?

At this stage, participants will probably want to see photographs of each other. Don't be in too much of a rush to offer this. Run an e-tivity on how a fixed photograph may give a stereotypical view of a participant, or of their personality or mood.

If you do go for photos or little videos at Stage 2, encourage people to post several in different moods and styles, with some personal commentary.

The student group will probably want to introduce some social media at this stage, if you haven't. Encourage participants to set up a personal profile and take responsibility for the networking for a social media course site if they wish. You can suggest some basic rules, for example, on inclusivity and avoidance of plagiarism.

Stage 3: Information exchange

At this stage e-tivities that can gradually encourage participants to take more personal responsibility for their active learning and interacting are helpful. In invitational messages, try to suggest and model strategies for active online learning. Most participants will still need help to handle masses of response messages and to find and personalize who and what they wish to work with. The moderator role-shifts from the 'host' role at Stage 2 to the archiving, summarizing and feedback role at Stage 3.

Great thinkers

Using the great thinkers from your disciplines can be great sparks for e-tivities. Here are some examples that we have tried:

- Start repositories of references and run an e-tivity so everyone contributes and comments. You could include TED (www.ted.com) and Kahn Academy (www.kahnacademy.org) videos if you wish. Your website will soon build up.
- Offer text, audio or video of great speeches. Participants condense them into 12 words, discuss the meanings and share them (use a micro-blog, perhaps).
- Suggest key concepts from your course for writing and sharing their own 'speech'. Maybe a little video of them presenting it (keep to two minutes).
- Ask for 'postcard' messages from one of the people from your discipline whom you admire; for example, individual explorers or inventors. (Twitter is the new 'postcard', or try text messages on mobiles.) How would participants respond?

- Considering the history of your discipline, are there more men or women mentioned in textbooks? Consider the implications and discuss them.
- Ask each participant to undertake a piece of research on a well-known figure from your discipline, and build an interest site. Start to introduce the importance of good referencing and evidencing.
- Ask participants to think of questions that they would like to ask and then to role-play interviewing each other as these figures. Post the results of the interviews for everyone to see.

Skills

Stage 3 is a good time and place for skill development. Try these:

- Find and try out keyboard tutors. See which increase typing speeds. Share the results of your research and see who can improve their typing speed.
- Practise summarizing information—for example, the theory of relativity—in 12 words.
- Practise summarizing sets of messages from Stages 2 and 3.
- Undertake 'compare and contrast' research. Develop a set of criteria for good or bad sites, or good or bad mobile apps for your course, or more or less relevant, or more or less useful. Then, using the criteria, each participant selects one and indicates how he or she would evaluate it. Encourage discussion and challenge.
- Ask each participant or small group to undertake research on a topic and report back to the group. Lead a plenary discussion on the results.

Compare

Investigating, comparing and contrasting electronic resources works really well at Stage 3:

- Investigate the best way for teams to work online, share ideas and evaluate them.
- Try out some online competitive and collaborative games.
- If you were advising a well-known writer from your discipline, what would you say about the layout and content of his or her book? What's missing? What's out-of-date? Each participant finds a free-to-use online resource or mobile app that might support one part of the course.
- Ask one participant to identify three websites or mobile apps of use to the group and post an evaluation of each one. Another participant then

visits each of the three and comments on the sufficiency of the evaluation, and adds his or her views and so on. The e-moderator summarizes. This works best on a wiki.

Preferred and viable futures

- Introduce a range of e-tivities to show how there is not just one future for your subject, but a range, some more desirable than others.
- Are there any scenarios about futures for your discipline? What are they called? Who thinks they offer a likely, viable or preferred view or less desirable futures?
- Try getting people to look back and gain insights . . . leading to foresight. (See the example timeline e-tivity on page 144.)
- Explore trends and extrapolate them.
- Investigate what happened to what appeared to be amazing innovations that failed.
- What happened suddenly and unexpectedly in your discipline and acted as a 'gamechanger'?

'Big' data sets

You might be wishing to introduce your participants to exploration of big data sets for your discipline. Now is the moment. However, we've found that small e-tivities where they explore subsets and share their findings with two or three others are a very good way in, and enable skills development in the platforms and opportunities. Set up help areas to reduce the pressure on help desks and encourage skills and techniques sharing.

Evaluation

Evaluation processes are usually good value for e-tivities.

- Try 'reversal'. What would happen if we did the opposite of what's advised by some authority?
- What are the 'seminal' books or papers for your areas of expertise? Why do you think they became so important? What's dropped away over the years and why?
- For your course, in what ways has online learning contributed or detracted from some criteria—say scalability, accessibility, costs?

Techniques

Debates

Try holding structured meetings (in, say, virtual classrooms) to reach decisions, such as:

- political debates;
- mock board meetings;
- lobby groups;
- voting on issues;
- discussion, buzz or focus groups;
- simulations or role-plays.

Take stances on key issues. For example, present a contentious issue: try 'introducing e-learning' or pick two sides of an argument for your topic. Divide participants into groups; for example, sceptics, wild enthusiasts, serious enthusiasts, pragmatists (it's going to happen, so how will we do it?). Run a plenary taking the key issues from each, and solutions. Try this in a virtual classroom where there are good voting tools.

Creative techniques

Here are some creative techniques:

- brainstorming;
- Delphi techniques;
- nominal group techniques;
- reversal;
- metaphors.

Promote 'out-of-the-box' thinking through simple e-tivity design:

- Imagine that better treatment for human bones and joints means that walking (Zimmer) frames are no longer needed. What could we do with all the Zimmer frames in the world?
- Try cybernetics (comparisons between human-made and biological objects). Offer a topic, and then each participant illustrates examples of five items from his or her desk. Try to 'force-fit' connections and see if they offer new insights into the topic.
- Start a 'round robin' story. Start by offering two sentences relevant to your course. Each participant adds a sentence.

- Investigate why we still use 'analogue' time, i.e. hours and minutes. How could the world go to digital time?

Questions

Try posting intriguing questions from any relevant topic of your choice. Or try to choose something that is simply one word or phrase. It works best if there are many different interpretations and perhaps a YouTube video, website or mobile app to explore. You will need very good summaries when the questions are answered and a plenary to explore the meaning and usefulness of the information.

For example, we asked these about the *Titanic*:

- Where do we get valid information from?
- Why was there such a belief in the unsinkable nature of the *Titanic*?
- How many people did a lifeboat hold (and why)?
- Where did the *Titanic* sail from?
- What kind of people were on board?
- Has the *Titanic* been raised from the sea?
- How many people survived the disaster? What kind of people were they?
- How many movies have been made about the sinking of the *Titanic*?
- What does the word 'titanic' mean?
- Who holds the rights to the sunken treasure?
- Who directed the film *Raise the Titanic*?
- Where is the *Titanic* museum?
- What was the name of the character that Kate Winslet played in one *Titanic* film?
- Did the captain go down with the ship?
- Who rescued the survivors?
- Can you play or sing any of the music from the last night of the *Titanic*?
- What did they eat on the last night?

Try getting participants to brainstorm questions as well as answers.

When I've run this, it's led on to a very wide range of discussions well beyond the 'facts', e.g. moral issues, gender relationships, weather forecasting, domino human errors, social class, historical perspectives, variability of the mass media and many more.

History harvests and artefacts

Encourage your participants to collect and contribute stories from their community history, especially with a picture of some artefact. These work brilliantly as sparks for all kinds of e-tivities and discussions and in different disciplines (Parry, 2012).

What if?

Stage 3 is a great moment to encourage 'out-of-the-box' thinking and have some fun. A good warm-up for more difficult knowledge sharing is to encourage participants to consider the extremes involved.

Ask what are the consquences if:

- the world ran out of paper;
- the Internet crashed;
- exams were banned;
- there were no university campuses;
- [add your own idea from your topic here . . . but think extreme].

If you and your participants wish, they can discuss the likelihood of the event happening, but the main purpose is to start extreme thinking about consequences.

Visitors

From Stage 3 onwards, you might want to introduce selective use of an 'outsider' such as a topic expert to the group, to stimulate discussion. To maximize the use of their time, build them into e-tivity processes and be specific about what you want them to do and when! Ask participants to practise their questioning and summarizing skills.

Stage 4: Knowledge construction

Your participants should be working well together by this point.

Structured teams

You can start to run 'snowball'-type e-tivities, with smaller groups merging into bigger ones. You can explore structures of effective work teams and specific roles such as chair, resource finder, recorder, summarizer, reviewer, critic and timekeeper. Try some action learning sets for e-tivities with participant-led e-moderating and team leading. If you haven't already, try out one or two new platforms for 'working together' (see pages 62–8).

Concepts

At this stage in a course or process, it's important to introduce conceptual models, ideas and theories for examination, exploration and application. In e-tivity processes, make it clear that the purpose of the e-tivity is not necessarily looking for consensus or closure, but wide exploration of issues.

- Take a key diagram, model or concept from your course or discipline. Ask each participant to apply it, or find examples. Compare and contrast between the examples offered. Draw it online and collectively improve it.
- Take a key concept and apply it in a new way.
- Take a key concept and demonstrate the extent to which it does or does not apply to a particular case example.

Positions

Participants can very usefully adopt a variety of 'positions' online to cover multiple perspectives. Here are some ideas:

- Take a key concept or model and explore how people belonging to different professions, such as that of physician, lawyer, politician or teacher, would apply it.
- Case studies and problem-based learning work well at this point.
- Introduce staged case-study information with questions.
- Introduce challenging problems with a variety of solutions.
- Ask participants to produce plans for action based on limited amounts of information—for example, a marketing plan, a business plan, a product launch.
- Use scenarios for the future. Offer two or three different cameos of how your discipline will look in the future: for example, different types of schools, new technologies for medicine, virtual performing arts. Prompt discussion on the adequacy and implications of these scenarios. If you've got a 3-D virtual world, you can create a new immersive environment and run virtual world e-tivities in it.

Summarizing

Encourage all forms of reviewing and summarizing:

- Ask individual participants, teams or groups to undertake investigation of one topic or area to contribute to a whole piece of work or report.
- Ask individual participants, teams or groups to undertake summarizing, critiquing and combining information.
- Offer e-tivities that rework ideas or discussions using techniques such as concept mapping.
- Encourage them to use all available media to offer summaries (e.g. in Twitter).

Stage 5: Development

At this stage, try to allow the maximum amount of choice. Ensure that all the summaries and archives are available for participants to use as resources. Accountability and responsibility are more important at this stage than 'content'. However, the usual approach to pacing and timescales should continue.

At this stage, I've suggested ideas that focus on self-reflection and evaluation of the learning. However, many of these approaches can also be used for teacher- or peer-led assessment. Almost all of them can form part of a written report or essay that can be used for formative or summative assessment. In this way the maximum amount of alignment between learning, planned learning outcomes, and assessment can be achieved.

Footprints

Offer essays, reports or collated Web or social media sites from previous students on the course (with permission or disguised, of course) and run an e-tivity on how participants would have marked, assessed and graded them.

Review

Offer e-tivities to consider the evaluation of both the learning that has occurred and the knowledge that has been generated. By all means, enable them to understand how to give constructive feedback.

- Try 360-degree evaluation or assessment—each participant asks another three participants specific questions about their experience of working together. Encourage participants to explore how they judge their success.
- Go back to expectations at the beginning of the course. Would participants change them if starting again? To what extent have their expectations been met and why?
- Would the group have worked differently if it had met physically too? If so, in what way?
- Encourage them to open up their e-portfolios (or part of them) to other learners for comments.

Technology

Explore the technology in use.

- If the group were designing an online environment, what would it need?
- What one new feature in the technology would have helped with learning?
- How did the participants succeed in spite of a barrier created by the technology?
- How would they put together the various platforms in use in the course to make them more personal, more inclusive, more accessible?

Reflections

Encourage reflection on the overall experience. Ask participants to use their e-portfolios or blogs if they have them.

- Ask participants to review one of their own messages and rework it to show how they would like it to appear now.
- Try asking for examples of various concepts to be picked out, or summaries or further conclusions to be drawn from earlier e-tivities.
- Ask for action plans—offer some structure and feedback.
- Ask for personal development plans—offer some structure and feedback.
- Give masses of feedback and constructive criticism. Encourage participants to offer this to each other, too.
- Ask individuals and groups to offer a 'footprint' (a piece of knowledge, new idea, special insight) to be offered to others starting the course afresh. Ask groups to agree the footprint statement between them.

- Ask participants to review all posted messages and to comment on what helped to move the discussion along and what did not.
- Ask participants to comment on the roles they each adopted.
- Ask participants to articulate the emotions they felt at various points in the course and why.

If developing skills in reflection is a purpose, try an activity which collects these reflections.

For example, ask each participant to summarize, from their perspective, what transpired during the e-tivity for him or her. Then they e-mail the summary to you as the e-moderator. After you've received them all, you can (with their permission) summarize and post them into a group area and ask them to discuss their respective perspectives and interpretations. At this point, either individual or group writing for assessment could take place.

If your participants understand a concept or topic better because of taking part in an e-tivity, you'll find that they will express satisfaction in the experience in some way. Try asking them what they would do differently as a result of taking part in the e-tivities as a form of assessment. You can also build this kind of self-assessment into an e-tivity. Your institutional LMS/VLE will offer the opportunity to embed feedback quizzes and tests into e-tivities. These can be useful to start an e-tivity off as a spark for discussion, or to give occasional fast feedback to participants as part of regular pacing.

Futures techniques

- Visioning;
- Scenario development;
- Trend analysis.

These are all easy to turn into e-tivities or e-tivities sequences. Lead discussions about impact, preferred and viable futures and how to create them rather than stand by and let them happen. This is very motivating and inspiring for participants.

Before and after!

Many good Stage 5 e-tivities can be set up and developed throughout the course. For example, ask participants to establish their understandings and share them at the very beginning, record them simply in an e-portfolio or personal space tool and then revisit them, and share key insights at this stage.

If these ideas are not enough, check out 'Futures Techniques' on Wikipedia or try Curt Bonk and Ke Zhang's (2008) book for even more learning activities ideas. There's more in Resources for Practitioners 2 and 3 as well.

Resources for practitioners 2

Creativity and e-tivities

Why should we try to be more creative and inventive in our e-tivities? Here is the response from one enthusiastic and successful e-tivity designer:

> E-learning got a bad name once . . . 'boring'! Many of our participants have experienced many courses, presentations and seminars and are used to skimming documents. We often now want them to learn in more depth. However, expecting people to concentrate in front of a computer over weeks, months and years is expecting a lot! Without the sense of fun, the sense of otherness, the sense of standing back, participants will only learn tips and tricks. But with the sense of wonder, they can change the way they think and work. As e-tivity designers we have to help create and sustain the sense of wonder. IW

This resource offers an overview of thinking and acting differently in the context of developing and e-moderating e-tivities. The idea is to introduce more fun and freedom into your e-tivities. A 'touch of creativity' in our e-tivities and our e-moderating work will delight our participants and we'll all have more fun and engagement.

By example and by influence, e-tivity designers can enable online participants to think and act more creatively, which is a most important attribute for everyone in this fast-changing century. Solving problems and innovating are unlikely to be successful if based on what worked in the past. We can model ways of doing things differently in our e-tivities and keep our teaching dynamic at the same time.

Thinking creatively involves breaking down and restructuring knowledge in order to secure new insights. Understanding how we have created that knowledge in our minds in the first place helps us to reorganize our thoughts.

The easiest way to start is by trying some techniques and learning for yourself. The only rule is that you need to take a little controlled risk from time to time. Preparation, however, is just as important as always. However, you might need to be sanguine about the precise outcome that you achieve. Go with the flow!

Creative thinking involves two main kinds of processes: divergent and convergent. Divergent thinking involves widening the thought processes around a specific issue and generating many ideas. To encourage divergent thinking it is important to remove constraints and structures and push away the usual boundaries. When the limits of divergent thinking seem to be reached, convergence can narrow down the possibilities and choices can be made. Convergent and divergent processes map closely onto the way we often design e-tivities. For example, we ask each participant to contribute some experience or an idea, we ask the group to keep building on them, then later we ensure that they are grouped or categorized and explored or explained in the plenary.

Here are some sparks for you to explore.

Images

Gareth Morgan, writing about metaphors and imaging, says, 'We are often trapped by the images we hold of ourselves' (Morgan, 2006). If we reconsider the image we have of ourselves with others, our colleagues, our participants, other stakeholders in e-tivities, and in a creative learning environment, we can break open the traps. We can create shared meanings and new ways of understanding and working with ideas. We can give energy and focus to the task of teaching and learning.

There is a story about a group of climbers who became badly lost in a severe snowstorm in Switzerland. They had nearly given up hope when one person found a map in his pocket. The group summoned up the last of their energy and found their way to safety. Only later was it discovered that the map was of the Pyrenees, not the Alps!

Where does your map of teaching and learning online come from? Has it been influenced by poor experiences as a learner or an online participant? Who or what was the most influence on creating your map of the way e-moderating works? Will it get you out of trouble or does it lead you constantly down new and exciting paths? What kind of impression will it give to others when you are in an online group? As an e-tivity designer, check out your own limitations and boundaries before you begin!

Metaphors

Metaphors in e-tivities give insights into everyday processes. These often lead to new ideas. We can use metaphors as sparks in e-tivities. They also work well in summaries to offer new insights to participants.

As I have been moving through my Masters I have begun to see how deeply connected Online Pedagogies and Learning Design are . . . though separate subjects in my curriculum, it seems that in fact you can't really have one without the other. E-tivities are the content, Learning Design is the sort of 'practical manual' or 'structure' in applying this content, that is derived from the knowledge and research developed by online pedagogical best practice. So if it were . . . let's say a sport metaphor: Online Pedagogy is the GAME . . . of football/netball and Learning Design is the Game PLAN. Learning Design is the coach in the locker room in those Hollywood 'football' films, scrawling strategies (e-tivities) for plans of moves in the game on a white board. Or something more creative perhaps? Dance? Online Pedagogy is the style of dance, Learning Design is the choreography, and e-tivities are the crowd-mesmerizing steps we all came to watch. PW

Here is a metaphor from one e-moderator. He was simultaneously taking part in one of our online courses to increase his e-moderating skills (and tutoring for an online Masters' programme):

I think the following metaphor applies to my online experience during the last month. The e-mod course has been like being lifted in a balloon on a clear day, with perfect weather conditions, so as to gain a colourful and friendly view of the e-moderating landscape. Now, my Masters course is like having to be one of the pilots on a transatlantic flight, needing to monitor carefully very sophisticated signals for the take-off and to ensure that everyone would feel confident enough that we would land safely eight months later having enjoyed an enriching long-term learning experience. Two very different contexts and time frames. Both challenging and valuable in their own ways. I wonder if I can introduce a balloon to the jet flight? PG

Here are some metaphors that the (UK) Open University tutors have suggested that gave them new insights into the e-moderating role.

The e-moderator as a football club manager

I've always thought of a football club manager when I think of the e-moderator's role. First of all, you have to get out on the coaching ground (the Web) and run some regular varied routines which develop new skills in your players (e-tivities). In between times you have to motivate the players (participants) through all their problems, and cope with those niggling little injuries when they can't seem to get the assessment on time.

Second, you have to deal with the whole team, from your expensive signings (those participants with lots of ability), your youth team products (the young students with lots of potential or those of any age new to online) and the free transfers (participants you may have doubts about but who get through somehow).

Third, you have to motivate the players (participants) after matches (e-tivities and assignments). You can praise those who've done well (carefully online), encourage those who've done reasonably (to bring out the best in them) and gently let those who've done badly know what they need to do to make the grade in this league.

Fourth, you have to deal with TV and the media (the writers and producers of the course and the e-tivities), who are continually looking for feedback and may not have experienced what it's like to play a team from the lower divisions (run an e-tivity with failing software), or to play a team stuffed full of internationals, unfamiliar with the home team's cultural ideas (inter-cultural course).

Fifth, you have to listen to the chairman (the monitor). Good monitors (like good chairmen of football clubs) don't second-guess what you do but do give helpful words of advice—which you need to listen to and take account of. They stay in the background and don't interfere too much but give timely advice. Bad chairmen (and monitors) always want to interfere and pick the team for you.

And finally, you yourself have to keep up-to-date with the latest developments in the game and in coaching (your subject, your e-moderating skills). You have to stand on cold, windswept terraces watching reserves for that jewel for the future (i.e. scour the journals for articles and write-ups that you can use as a spark). PS

Financial investment

As e-moderators we have relatively little face-to-face contact with participants, compared with a conventional teaching situation. We compensate with e-tivities, assignments, e-mail and telephone contact. So we have to maximize our effectiveness at these moments. Participants will, on their own, read the course and understand a good deal of it. Our added value as e-moderators is to every so often test their understanding, help bring out the true issues, consolidate what has been learned, question the theory. This is putting a little money aside every so often, providing added value at a good moment in a useful way. Thus I see my role of weaving, archiving and summarizing as the interest on their investment. KL

Chrysalis to butterfly

At the beginning of the course, participants emerge from the chrysalis (of logging on), blinking around in the light. At first, participants flit all over the garden (platform) and the e-moderator's role is to enable them to fly in formation towards flowers of knowledge at particular times (e-tivities) and then, looking splendid, wings furled, go into the exam! Thereafter the lifecycle begins again. SG

Online groups as choirs

Choirs have to be coached and taught how to read music (Stages 1 and 2 of the model). They need very regular rehearsals (e-tivities). Some sing only in a group, others are solo artists (issues of participation, lurking, vicarious learning). They need at Stages 3 and 4 to work together. In the end they give a wonderful final performance and have all enjoyed the experience (Stage 5). (Yes—some do sing out of tune, and some very flat!) JA

Piggy banks

I see the mind of a participant as a piggy bank. There is a slot for ideas, experiences, concepts, suggestions to enter (through taking part in e-tivities). Sometimes they will enter easily; sometimes it may be necessary to ease the slot open a little: to take larger coins, perhaps from another country, or folded notes, in the event of real riches (contingent e-moderating). Getting things out may also be a varied experience. Sometimes there is a lock and a little key, which can be fine if we have not lost the key. Others have a little plastic snap-on cover which we may need to prise off carefully. If this doesn't work, we may need to use a tool. If that is no good either, we may need someone else to help us. Having travelled that route, we may then reflect on how much easier it would have been if we had asked for some help a little earlier (role of emotions and time).

Sometimes there may seem to be no apparent way of extracting the contents at all. Then we may need to go back to the slot and see if we can slip something in there which can be used to ease things out again (IT help?). Or, we may need to try to create a totally new way in, so that all the goodies inside can flow out freely (revamp the e-tivity). If we do not want everything to cascade out all at once, we may need to fit a tap or two; or perhaps a little door, and for this one, we will look after the key carefully (managing contribution). PC

Knowledge circulation

I find it helps to picture knowledge as a circulatory system, rather like the human blood circulation system. The components of blood are many and varied, and derive from a number of sources. Some of these are internal, such as hormones (contributions from other participants), some of them external, such as food (spark and websites). Knowledge enters into the bloodstream in a similar way. If things are not going well, attempts may be made to inject the knowledge (give additional information, assess). It circulates around with pumps to help (the e-moderator!) and serves a critical life-giving purpose for the person concerned. GK

Can you try metaphors in your e-tivities?

Another common way to stimulate ideas is to consider objects that encapsulate or represent activities, ideas and processes.

Mission to Mars

For your subject, run a wiki-tivity asking learners to imagine gathering together the contents of a time capsule that will be opened in 100 years by future professionals of the industry or sector.

The capsule can include five elements, metaphorical (e.g. 'patience') or literal (e.g. 'a degree certificate'), that future professionals of the industry should acquire.

And five mistakes that should never be repeated!

This idea also works well as a Stage 2 e-tivity. Or try it with key issues of a year from your discipline, or this week's news from around the world.

Reversal

By turning a situation or problem around and looking at it differently, we often get fresh and interesting new perspectives or ideas. A frequently used creative technique is 'reversal'. For example, try: 'How can we make group e-tivities more boring?'

Here are some ideas:

- Always lecture, one-way transmission.
- Never make your objectives clear.

- Single individuals out and demand answers to your questions.
- Talk endlessly about your own experience without relating it back to the concepts in the course.
- Intervene regularly, and answer your own messages.

Did you think of many others?

Now take your list and reverse the ideas—you have a simple list of good practice. For example:

- Plan activities and involvement of everyone.
- Ensure the online environment is suitable and have plenty of pacing and breaks.
- Be clear about outcomes expected, timings and process.
- Support the group process as a whole, avoiding unnecessary interventions.
- Use only appropriate and clear teaching sparks, links and references.
- Plan examples and illustrations carefully.

New ideas from combining

Do you get the idea? You could try reversal and then re-reversal now: 'How can we ensure that novice computer users do not become fully comfortable with electronic learning?' and 'How can we use assignment marking to undermine students' confidence?'.

Can you try out one of these ideas with your participants in one of your e-tivities? Make a note of how you felt about trying this and what the participants' responses were. Could you see the divergent and convergent phase? Most importantly, can you see whether they were thinking a little differently, a little more creatively than usual? Were they all fully engaged in the task? Did they comment on their own ways of learning as well as the outcome from the task?

Resources for practitioners 3

Using other people's digital materials (OERs)

Information professionals spend their working lives advising on the use of materials I'm to cover in one resource.

What follows are some 'rules of thumb' that might give you more confidence and fabulous sparks.

1   You need to understand how you *can* use other people's digital material in your design and delivery of e-tivities.

2   Check before you take . . . most sites say what you can do with the materials on the site. If they don't, you might be able to make some reasonable assumptions based on the information that follows.

3   Always acknowledge the author, contributors and source. Why not be generous? And it is good practice too.

4   Always consider a resource that is already available and that you can legally and ethically embed as a spark in e-tivities, before producing your own. Put your time and effort into designing wonderfully engaging e-tivities if you can, rather than producing more material.

5   If you need to produce something to use in your e-tivities, make it available to others for their online teaching if you can. You will reap

the rewards and know you are contributing to the pool of learning resources.

6   Use your e-tivities to enable your participants to understand the right ways of using other people's material too.

There are many ways you can secure online resources to use as a spark.

Copyright   Copyright law applies to the digital environment. Copyright material in digital form is protected in the same way as material in any other format. For example, text and images on a website are protected by copyright in the same way as printed material. If it's something you really want to use and someone else owns the copyright, seek permission. You may be able to legally reproduce or communicate copyright material in some circumstances under exceptions contained in copyright legislation, or through an explicit or implicit licence from the copyright owner accompanying the material. They might want to charge you, but they might just appreciate your asking.

Creative Commons licences   Creative Commons (CC) is an organization that provides ready-made licensing agreements which are less restrictive than the 'all rights reserved' terms of standard international copyright. Owners of material and creators can decide if they want to apply CC licences to their works. There are several CC licence types, and you need to be sure that the material you are using has a licence that meets your needs. The CC website (creativecommons.org) provides advice on what licence to use if you want to publish your own work in this way and also on what the different licences mean. For example, the simplest licence just requires you to attribute the work to its author and then you can use it freely.

Open educational resources   You can find many stable, searchable and growing repositories of CC and free-to-use materials, usually called open educational resources (OERs). You can also search many sites for material licensed under CC, for example, Flickr, Wikipedia, YouTube.

The best-known site, which has been around since 2002, is that of MIT's open courseware, which started it all (www.ocw.mit.edu). The open courseware from Massachusetts Institute of Technology (MIT) is provided on the Web under a CC licence BY-NC-SA, which requires attribution, non-commercial use, and requires materials that are derived from them to be CC licensed in the same way.

The OER movement has now spawned many more stable repositories. Do make a start on taking a look for yourself on oercommons.org and jorum.ac.uk. Or ask around in your professional or disciplinary community.

Images Images are a special case because there are so many images, and so many with open licences. For example, Flickr has hundreds of millions of images with open CC licences (put a tick in the box for CC content— you'll find it under 'advanced search'). Google Image search also has an advanced search facility where you can filter a search so that it only includes results for images you can freely use.

Special educational agreements Many countries and educational institutions like universities have special arrangements and provide resources on a stable, searchable internal repository site, usually behind the institution's firewall. Resources on these sites can be used and linked within your LMS/VLE for educational purposes, depending on the licence.

For example, many universities and colleges maintain a database of teaching materials that is securely located behind the institution's log-in controls and is accessible to staff. It enables them to share material in related areas and deliver teaching materials across multiple teaching and delivery channels. Where I'm currently working, Swinburne University of Technology, we have a searchable (safe) place to deposit and access teaching resources called Swinburne Commons. This provides continuity of material development over time (regardless of changes in staff) and an easy way of linking sparks into our online and blended learning programmes.

Sometimes they are a well-kept secret, so ask if you have one, and, if not, why not?

Textbooks There is a move to provide free open textbooks, particularly by governments, with the goal of reducing the cost of textbooks. For example, in British Columbia (BC, Canada) the BC Campus provides access to a repository of course materials, shareable online learning resources (SOLR), for post-secondary education, and this has now become a state open-textbook programme. Other locations, for example Openstax College, provide open access to textbooks. It is supported by large charitable foundations (Gates, Hewlett) and is a non-profit organization. Openstax textbooks are licensed under CC 'attribution'.

Open repositories for research articles Most scholarly articles are in proprietary databases, which require subscriptions. But, more recently, open repositories have come into being. They offer access to scholarly journal articles. These are not usually openly licensed but they do include millions of scholarly articles and book chapters, which can be freely accessed, and therefore can be *linked to* (see 'Linking' below). What's more, the content of open repositories can be readily located, since they use a common Web protocol, which enables them to be located through Google Scholar (www.scholar.google.com.au). Try it! I find it's best to use the 'advanced search' to get what you want—it's pretty easy.

Wikipedia   Don't forget Wikipedia, one of the great achievements of the Web. All Wikipedia content bears a CC licence, and can be freely used. You need to make sure that the content is appropriate and of adequate quality for your purposes. What is more, Wikipedia has given rise to Wikimedia Commons—which is a vast online resource (15 million items at the end of 2012) that can be freely used.

Linking   You can also use anything online as long as you *link to it*, rather than copying it. Linking is fine in copyright terms in almost all jurisdictions, and is *not* a copyright infringement (that is, something that is the exclusive right of the copyright owner). You can link to Web content in cases where *copying* it may be a breach of the copyright owner's rights.

I also hope you'll benefit as an e-tivity designer by using materials into which others have put their knowledge and care—and will subsequently want to share more of your own work in this way too.

Many thanks to Derek Whitehead of Swinburne University of Technology for his invaluable help with this resource.

DESIGNING E-TIVITIES

Resources for practitioners 4

First-time
e-tivity designer
and e-moderator

Designing the e-tivity

Richard works in a human developmental role for a large distributed organization. He was charged with running a series of activities for 10 team leaders to promote electronic group working and learning together across the company. He wanted to ensure that the activities were not just about e-communication but also had some relevance, usefulness and authenticity. He approached me for help with his first attempt and I offered him the outline of suggestions in Tables 1.1 and 1.2 (pages 2 and 3) and agreed to comment on his e-tivity design. What follows are Richard's attempts at his first e-tivity design with some commentary from me. Further on you can read what happened when the e-tivity was delivered.

Richard decided to try a free version of a learning management system (LMS) that included a wiki, a synchronous chat and a virtual classroom, which neither he nor the participants had used before.

Richard's first attempt at an e-tivity

Version 1: Cost-saving measures, a wiki-tivity

TITLE   Pie Slicing, Costs Saving and Consensus.

PURPOSE   To identify, share and evaluate ideas that respond to a particular situational challenge.

SPARK   The Board has announced that the worsening economic situation warrants a range of corporate cost reduction initiatives. The Board stresses that it wishes to exclude down-sizing its workforce at this time, preferring instead to engage that workforce in the identification of feasible cost reduction areas that everyone can adopt.

TASK   You are to propose, share and evaluate five cost reduction initiatives that can be implemented across the organization and that (as far as possible) impact no particular group or business unit more significantly than any other.

SCHEDULE and TIMING

The schedule will commence at 09:00 on Monday.

Each individual's five cost reduction proposals (facets of business activity) are to be posted to the wiki by 17:00 on Wednesday.

Students will pair up by 08:00 on Thursday and post notice of their partnerships in the group mailbox before that time.

Between 08:00 on Thursday and 08:00 on Friday, each pair will then consider all of their joint (10 in total) proposals and reach consensus as to which five they propose taking forward to the next stage of the exercise.

Between 08:00 on Friday and 08:00 on Sunday each student pair will expand each of their five chosen proposals by identifying three subordinate cost reduction initiatives under each general area/proposal.

These expanded proposals will be mounted to the wiki by 12:00 on Sunday.

Between 12:00 on Sunday and 18:00 on Wednesday of week 2, each pair will critically examine the proposals from other student pairs and post comments on their viability, feasibility and possible opportunities for improvement.

At 18:00 on Thursday—and lasting for two hours—the group will convene in the virtual classroom to discuss the exercise and its outcomes.

Gilly's comments to Richard

● I quite like the title and purpose but maybe you could go back to them later to ensure they are as enticing as they could be. Could the Board's instruction be a bit more workforce friendly? To keep the relevance and authenticity, maybe you could commit to offering something to the Board as an outcome for the contributions and collaboration of the e-tivity?

- The spark looks pretty good to me; I'd like to have a try at it anyway!
- I think I understand the sequencing and scheduling but this needs to be laid out better, with deadlines. Could you arrange to text them or post deadlines and reminders from the schedule into their diaries?
- You will need to make it clear what you, as the e-moderator, will do and when.
- There are no instructions on how to find your partner.
- Do they already know how to use the wiki? There would need to be a direct link. It's good to give them the framework in the wiki to make both first and later responses clearer.
- I suggest you specify the length of responses that you're expecting (this could get very big and too long), and maybe post a couple of examples on the wiki to demonstrate both the content and brevity of what you are expecting.
- I assume you'll be there at the end for the virtual classroom—it would be good to make this clear.
- You say you are going to monitor their engagement. This might worry me. What will be the nature of this and any implications?
- Some of your language is a bit 'school-masterish'. Perhaps you could soften it and present yourself more as a facilitating peer or colleague? I prefer to call people taking part 'participants' rather than students.
- Will you get everyone to come into the virtual classroom after work on the last Thursday? Maybe move to office hours?

Richard's e-tivity: Final invitation

Here's what Richard's e-tivity looked like when it became an invitation:

Sequence	1.1 Commence on Monday morning, please.
Title	Slices of Pies
Purpose	To work together to critically evaluate ideas about cost savings, with a 360-degree consensus flavour.
Spark	The Board has announced that 'the worsening economic situation warrants a range of corporate cost reduction initiatives. The Board stresses that it wishes to exclude down-sizing its workforce at this

	time; preferring instead to engage that workforce in the identification of feasible cost reduction areas that everyone can adopt.' <link to video with Chairman of Board speaking about the context of internal cost reduction>
Task	Propose, share and evaluate five cost reduction initiatives that can be implemented across the organization and which impact no particular group or business unit more significantly than any other.
1st response (individual)	Individually, consider and come up with five cost reduction ideas and post your bulleted list to the wiki by 17:00 (GMT) on Wednesday <link to wiki>. If you need inspiration, click here <link to Web and YouTube videos on cost savings ideas>. One or two lines maximum for each idea please, at this stage.
2nd response (pairs)	On Wednesday evening, I (Richard) will post a list of the pairs for working together. Between 08:00 on Thursday and 08:00 on Friday, each pair should consider their joint (total of 10) proposals and reach a negotiated agreement (by e-mail or whatever means suits you) through dialogue, and decide on five to take forward to the next stage of our e-tivity.
3rd response (pairs)	Between 08:00 on Friday and 08:00 on Sunday, in pairs, identify three action initiatives for each of your five proposals (15 in total). Post these to the wiki <link to wiki>.
4th response (pairs)	Between 12:00 on Sunday and 18:00 on Wednesday (week 2), each pair is to critically examine the expanded proposals from all other participant pairs; numerically score them and post comments on their viability, feasibility and possible opportunities for improvement. The wiki will have additional columns prepared ready for this exercise. *Scoring*—each of the five proposals can earn a maximum score of 15 points. You can amend and update your entries until Wednesday of week 2, but the table will then be locked.
5th response (all)	At 10:00 on Thursday of week 2—and lasting for 1.5 hours—all convene in the virtual classroom for the plenary session to discuss the exercise, its outcomes and the lessons learned.
Richard's availability and input	I will offer an opportunity to discuss your first ideas from 08.00 to 10.00 on Monday of week 1. I'll be in the chat box from time to time to stimulate your efforts and encourage you all to complete the stages of the schedule on time. I'll be available for the plenary session in the virtual classroom at the end. I will post the key learning points to emerge from the whole exercise. I will report outcomes back to the Board.
Schedule and time	I've posted key dates, reminders and schedule to your e-diaries.
Next	I'll remind you to move on to our next e-tivity as soon as 'Slices of Pies' is complete.

What happened

Richard becomes an e-moderator—his diary

Saturday (T minus 2 days before e-tivity start)
This is my first as a 'solo' e-moderator so I feel a certain sense of trepidation as I ready myself for the start. A small hiccup in the set-up arrangements or my inept incompetence has resulted in some problems with the self-registration system.

I have thought about just how much lead as the e-moderator I should give to the participants. Should I provide an example of a potentially suitable cost-saving idea to all participants, or would this shape or influence some of their ideas and restrict their scope and ingenuity? Similarly, I wonder whether the first participants to post their cost-saving ideas will shape and influence the thinking of the others. I opted not to provide an example unless participants need and ask for my help. My trepidation starts to smoulder.

Sunday (T minus 1 day before course start)
Since yesterday I've explored the course site a little more. I've discovered the way I can enrol participants. Phew, phew (two sighs of relief—one from me and one from the participants concerned!). I may have discovered the way to form the participants into groups. I cannot test this out yet. Hope they find their way in before tomorrow. There is now a small orange glow beneath my trepidation to accompany the smouldering of yesterday!

I have now laid out my own schedule (on paper!) for the e-tivity and it hangs on the wall above my computer screen for easy access and reference. *But* I am a very left-brain kind of guy. This depicts each day of the e-tivity, the details and duration of each of the participant tasks that will be undertaken during the e-tivity and notes of my interactions throughout the e-tivity. Constructing this and placing it close by has been a very therapeutic activity— my pulse rate and blood pressure have returned to normal.

Monday (T minus 0: e-tivity start day)
A little slowly, but with increasing frequency, my participants arrived in the course environment, seemingly none the worse for wear after the registration and enrolment process. The participants are busy working people. It's clear that this e-tivity challenge must be accommodated and woven into their hectic working lives.

I had conversations with three different individuals via the instant messenger chat facility. I have added a couple of general messages of guidance to the course home page and have received the first individual's five cost-savings ideas submitted to the correct wiki site. The fire beneath my trepidation appears to have gone out!

At around 17:00 today I realized that I had not stepped out of the office all day. Like a fussy mother hen I have been overly concerned about my participants and my imagination of their need for my help. Actually, other than for the chat conversations, which were not of the emergency type at all— rather just an exploration of how the service worked—there have been no panicky communications and I was worrying unnecessarily. There is a real lesson here!

Tuesday (T plus 1, second day of e-tivity)
The Task 1 wiki page has rapidly filled with each participant's initial five cost-saving proposals. I have grouped the participants into pairs, ahead of schedule, based on alphabetical order of the letters of their first names, and notified all participants of the pair groups that they belong to by e-mail. I needed a little more skill than I had to do this from within the LMS using its own 'Groups' function—something that will need addressing for the future. This lack of competence with the system tools may deprive me and the participants of some other functions and capabilities of the system, such as scoring each other's ideas. The lesson to draw from this is that e-moderators need to be fully conversant with the capabilities and tools of the system if they are to dispense the maximum benefit and experience to their participants.

Otherwise, the participants are coping admirably and are ahead of the intended schedule. This e-tivity could probably be shortened by one day but there may be more time savings to be had, so I shall evaluate that again later.

Wednesday (T plus 2, third day of e-tivity)
Each participant should have submitted their five cost saving suggestions to the wiki by 17:00 today, but all have already done so by 11:00.

I now believe that I had a set of tasks that are far more complex than they need to be. With the advantage of the spare time in the schedule now, I have decided to simplify tasks 2 to 4 and to notify the participants immediately. I will need to get the grid on the second wiki page changed to accommodate the simpler task and scoring design.

Thursday (T plus 3, fourth day of e-tivity)
I am waiting for technical support to develop a new grid for the wiki. Is that smoke I sense again?

All OK—grid was managed superbly and the participant pairs fell upon it with gusto and submitted the ideas to it almost before the ink on the grid was dry! Fire out—again!

Friday (T plus 4, fifth day of e-tivity)
It's 09:30 am and I have been into the system to check on the participants' progress and their achievement of Task 2, the deadline for which was 08:00 this morning. All the participant pairs have completed Task 2, and most have completed Task 3 (identification of three cost-reduction initiatives linked to each of their two major ideas) *and* submitted them to the new grid. Wow! What a superb bunch of people—way up on the schedule and clearly very enthusiastic and engaged. This is the second indication that the e-tivity could be shortened—probably by another day. Or I could have run another e-tivity simultaneously perhaps.

Only three participants have opted to invoke and set up the chat function. It's been nice to chat to these three from time to time—if only to help me feel comfortable about their experiences.

2nd Saturday (T plus 5, sixth day of e-tivity)
I am very pleased with the progress made by the participants. They have worked well in their pairs and with one minor exception all have managed to stay with the pace, often completing tasks before their due date and commencing the next task before its start date.

One participant told me she felt the schedule of the e-tivity should be a little more generous. The other participants have stayed with the pace or exceeded it. It's difficult therefore to draw design conclusions at this stage. There appear to be no other reported problems.

Will today start work on my preparations for the final session when I hope to provide feedback to the participants. This session will be conducted within the virtual classroom environment so am expecting to conduct a slide show, talking head with my voice and text chat. Eeek!

2nd Sunday (T plus 6, seventh day of e-tivity)
This morning a quick check of participants' progress against the schedule has revealed that I have another pair who have not completed Task 3 by the deadline of 08:00. Given this additional evidence I have messaged all participants with my decision to extend the deadline for Task 3 until tomorrow at noon, i.e. Monday of week two.

I recognize that I made no distinction between weekdays and weekend days when planning and setting out my timetable—on reflection I should have, more wisely, built a schedule that did not include coursework at weekends. These participants are all working at day jobs and my schedule may have invaded their private time a little too much.

2nd Monday (T plus 7, eighth day of e-tivity)
All participants have now completed Task 3 and several pairs have already entered their scores against other teams' submissions. With the rest of today and Tuesday and Wednesday yet to come, I sense that we are back on track and will be ready for Thursday's plenary session.

I have today also issued reminders to all participants that they will need to install, test, set up and familiarize themselves with the virtual classroom application we will be using for Thursday's plenary session. I too will need the intervening time to familiarize myself with this platform and to prepare my summary slide show for upload in good time.

2nd Tuesday to 2nd Wednesday (T plus 8 and 9, ninth and tenth days of e-tivity)
Participants' work and contribution to Task 4 (scoring the other teams' submissions) progresses well. This note is written late pm on Wednesday and I am waiting for only one team's scoring allocation. All other scores are in.

I have downloaded and installed the virtual classroom software, tested it and set up my audio arrangements. The slide presentation has been uploaded. I'm now confident that I can run the plenary at least in a basic fashion for tomorrow.

The last team submitted their scores by early evening and all is now set for tomorrow. I wait to see how much difficulty participants have with the virtual classroom functions, but there is already evidence that some have been in and explored its capabilities.

2nd Thursday (T plus 10, last day of e-tivity)
Today the e-tivity closes with a plenary session, scheduled to last up to 1.5 hours, which will utilize the virtual classroom application. With an hour to go before this session starts, I have uploaded my slide show and note that several participants have clearly already been in to explore.

Session went well, though chat facility not particularly busy with student questions during my slide presentation; there were one or two good questions at the end. I sense I didn't really engage the participants sufficiently to extract from them their reflections of the e-tivity but have e-mailed them all to encourage this—and there is to be a survey sent out to them in a week or so.

Summary of the Slices of Pie participant feedback from an electronic survey (received and written by Gilly)

Most participants enjoyed taking part and found the spark and introductions interesting. One definitely said he wasn't really interested in cost savings as a topic (although he contributed well). They felt they had communicated creatively with each other and with the e-moderator, including with people they had seen around the office but never spoken to before.

They understood what was required of them and most felt there was time to achieve the tasks, though one was unsure about this and another said she needed to work 'out-of-hours' to complete them. Another noted (with approval) that Richard made minor adjustments both to the design of the e-tivity and the deadlines whilst it was in progress. The participants' suggestions for improvement were that they would have been happy with more complex tasks. They also felt that they would have liked more of a snowball effect, e.g. from working in pairs to fours and beyond.

On the virtual classroom plenary, they felt that they received a good summary of the topic but they would have liked more opportunities to contribute for themselves at this point. One or two were distracted by the text chat in the virtual room.

Richard's final reflections

The e-tivity required mainly pairs working until the final group plenary. Whilst there were benefits in the participants practising electronic working and getting to know people they didn't know before, I could enhance this component in future. When I run this again I shall increase the complexity by moving the participants from singletons initially, to pairs and then finally to two groups for the final stages. There is also a need to give the participants the opportunity, through a further stage, to reflect on their prior proposals and to alter them if they think that's appropriate. This could be stimulated by my provision of a mid-way presentation. I would focus on elevating the original ideas so that cost saving initiatives become more meaningful and relevant. So I will merge them into two larger groups for the final stages, even though this will make the e-itivity more complex . . . if I'm clear about the instructions, I think it will work.

Next time I will accommodate some weekend breaks in the schedule—not everyone appreciated working seven days a week.

I sense that my participants would have benefited from an example from me in the early stages. This is because unless you can get a sufficiently 'big picture' idea at this early stage, it becomes more difficult to identify the subordinate or underlying contributory cost savings initiatives that are associated with the big idea. Or, to get more gradual engagement, this is probably the subject of a separate and earlier wiki-tivity.

For the plenary session I recognize that the process was too one-sided (me talking to the participants). I should have used it to get commentary, feedback and observations about experience from the participants. I will rectify this next time. I am gaining experience as an e-moderator as well as an e-tivity designer!

By the way, in addition to the collaboration benefits, there were authentic outcomes that might have been hard to achieve in any other way. There were worthy and potentially significant proposals that emerged from the e-tivity that will go to the Board for their consideration. They will be presented to the Board's next general meeting, with an acknowledgement of the contributions from the e-tivity group. The proposals included:

- energy consumption and thus cost reduction initiatives;
- more efficient and effective space utilization and commercialization opportunities;
- the deployment of low-cost technologies to virtualize meetings, and thereby reduce travel and communications costs;
- the centralization and aggregation of some business processes and functions to realize benefits of scale discounts and efficiencies;
- the formation of collaborative consortia with other organizations with similar business needs, to negotiate beneficial and cost-effective arrangements and prices with common suppliers.

Many thanks to 'Richard' for his work, open reflections and insights.

Resources for practitioners 5

E-tivity exemplars

Example A

Numbering, pacing and sequencing	*Put your e-tivity stage number and sequence number here*
Title	Escapology
Purpose	Understanding the impact of signage on escape route design and human behaviour in emergencies. This e-tivity will help you to form small groups. It will be useful for next week's multiple-choice quiz.
Brief summary of overall task	Capture and post a short video or brief series of visual examples of emergency signs and routes from your workplace or a public place (e.g. airport or train station), share and discuss it with others.
Spark	Videos of successful rescues (e.g. Hudson River aircraft). Use news footage of recent authentic examples. Or use movie clips.
Individual contributions	Post to the wiki <link> a video or two or three photos of signage and escape routes. Post a brief description of the place captured. Post by <date>.
Dialogue begins	In the wiki, ask questions and comment on at least two other people's videos or pictures. Form groups of three and collectively discuss the core similarities, differences and surprises. By Friday <date and time>, as a group of three, post at least five examples of very good practice, and five examples of poor practice, that you have identified.
E-moderator interventions	Summary from the e-moderator will be posted on Monday. (Notes for e-moderator: comment on the sufficiency of the group posts, adding additional examples if appropriate and relate directly to concepts of the course.)
Schedule and time	Total of 10 days (elapsed calendar time) from the start, in three parts. Expect to take about 40 minutes to capture your video or pictures, 30 minutes to post them, 60 minutes to look at and consider the contributions and 60 minutes to discuss, come up and post with your examples. So about two hours spread out over the 10 days' elapsed time.
Next	Please now move onto e-tivity 3, Living routes.

This e-tivity is good for Stage 2—it gets people posting and sharing quickly. It works well for psychology, design, built environment and engineering students, and many others. It often generates some humour and fun despite the seriousness of the topic.

Example B

Numbering, pacing and sequencing	Put your e-tivity stage number and sequence number here.
Title	Get me out of here
Purpose	Apply and test understanding of emergency signage and routes. This will help you in next week's quiz.
Brief summary of overall task	Take part in a simulated experience of escape and consider what you've learnt.
Spark	Briefly review the e-moderator summary from previous e-tivity 'Escapology' (see Example A opposite). (You need to simulate this safely—one way might be in a virtual 3-D world, e.g. Second Life or other simulated environment. Or you could ask your performing arts or design students to help you. The simulated location could be a submarine, oil rig, mine, fishing boat, aircraft or cruise ship.)*
Individual contributions	Take part in the 'escape' exercise. Then post one message to the bulletin board/forum <link> saying whatever you wish about your feelings or your learning from taking part.
Dialogue begins	Provide support to others and share understanding of the consequences.
E-moderator interventions	Summarize and weave all contributions.
Schedule and time	Total calendar/elapsed time allowed for this e-tivity, completion date, estimated total study time required (e.g. 2 x 1 hour).
Next	Link to next e-tivity.

This e-tivity is suitable for Stages 3 or 4. It was designed for psychology students but also works well for architecture, built environment, oil, gas and mining, the public sector and design, and perhaps also communications and events. It illustrates sequencing and scaffolding of e-tivities.

Example C

Numbering, pacing and sequencing	Put your e-tivity stage number and sequence number here.
Title	Connection correction
Purpose	Practising development of agile responses to real-life problems, using visualizing and diagramming techniques. Will help you with all future assignments and exams.
Brief summary of overall task	Using the technique 'multiple cause diagramming' (tutorial X), you will analyse a system capacity problem with your learning group (*of four and five—already established*) and identify a range of mitigating interventions to a real-life problem.
Spark	The Chief Information Officer (CIO) for the University asks for your help: 'Student complaints regarding poor quality and/or intermittent wireless connectivity to the Internet from the library have reached unacceptable levels. The complaints peak during high footfalls in the library. We need to solve this problem quickly as the semester begins soon. You may wish to investigate the available bandwidth options, the numbers of wireless-based stations that are deployed, the typical numbers of simultaneous wireless devices in use at any one time and the students' approaches to using the wireless resources.'
Individual contributions	Review the video notes on multi-cause diagramming <link here>. Register on and do the practice tutorials on <visualizing and diagramming social media tool>. Complete by day 2 of this e-tivity. Post any problems and solutions during your practice to the diagramming wiki <link here>.
Dialogue begins	In small groups, undertake a full-scale diagramming multi-cause activity. Complete this activity by day 5. Investigate the causal factors generated by your multi-cause diagram and create at least three options to recommend to the CIO. Indicate high, low and medium costs, impact on students and time required to implement solutions. Complete by day 8 and post to the Facebook site <link here>.
E-moderator interventions	On day 8, I will meet with the CIO to get his or her feedback and post his or her responses.
Schedule and time	Total of eight days (elapsed calendar time) from the start, in three parts. We estimate that you'll need to spend a bit of time organizing yourself and a total of up to four hours over the week.

Example C . . . continued

Numbering, pacing and sequencing	*Put your e-tivity stage number and sequence number here.*
Next	Please now move on to e-tivity 4, in your same groups. <link to a more complex e-tivity>

This e-tivity is good for Stages 3 or 4. You might like to try a fairly straight problem first at Stage 3 and go onto more complicated ones for Stage 4. For example, for Stage 4, you could remove the guidance from the last sentence in the brief's 'spark' text.

This e-tivity works well for entirely remote students or they can be co-located for the diagramming and action planning. It was developed originally for university-level IT students, with the university's CIO as the 'client', but works well for almost any discipline with suitably complex and authentic problems.

Example D

Numbering, pacing and sequencing	*Put your e-tivity stage number and sequence number here.*
Title	Back to the future
Purpose	Appreciate foresight and explore trends. This e-tivity directly leads to a graded assignment based on the last two weeks' work.
Brief summary of overall task	Create, contribute and explain a time line from a technology of your choice, work with your group to explore trends and insights and present a foresight to the plenary session. Download the timeline software and practise first <link>.
Spark	Review my short lecture on hindsight, insight and foresight, and the impact of trends here <link>. View my timeline and comments about the 'telegraph to the Internet'. <link to an example timeline>
Individual contributions	Choose one technology that was first adopted somewhere in the world at some point in the last 1,000 years. Create a timeline showing at least 10 critical events with their points in time. Add your timeline to the wiki, against your name, and in column 2 write a maximum of 150 words indicating what you've learned about trends from compiling it. Complete your individual timeline and posting by next Monday at the latest.
Dialogue begins	From Tuesday, in your groups of six, discuss the insights from your six individual timelines, and identify any common or linking attributes that characterized the 10 events. Choose one technology (or combine them, if appropriate), and prepare a five minute presentation on the future for your chosen technology as a result of the application of these characteristics and attributes. Include your insights into where and in what ways your chosen technology might have an impact five years from now. Upload the presentation to the wiki by Saturday.
E-moderator interventions	I will comment on all the group Prezi presentations by Wednesday. 10 marks will be awarded for the quality of your individual work and 10 for your group thinking, insights and presentation.
Schedule and time	Total of 10 days (elapsed calendar time) from the start, in three parts: individual, group discussions and preparation of presentation. I'd expect this total e-tivity to take you at least seven hours in total.

Example D . . . continued

Numbering, pacing and sequencing	*Put your e-tivity stage number and sequence number here.*
Next	Please now move onto e-tivity 3, Out of the blue.

This e-tivity is good for Stage 3 for many different disciplines. This example was for education students but I've seen it work well for IT, politics and conflict studies, medicine and health sciences, business, organizational development, transport and design of all kinds. Visual arts students enjoy providing more images on the timeline—why not?

If appropriate, the next e-tivity in the sequence can explore barriers to the adoption of promising innovations or less 'predictable' events.

Example E

Numbering, pacing and sequencing	Put your e-tivity stage number and sequence number here.
Title	Mirror, mirror on my screen . . .
Purpose	To prepare you to apply your new-found knowledge and wisdom and create new futures. This e-tivity will help you with the 'reflections' section of your final assignment.
Brief summary of overall task	Taking part in this course has brought you to a new place—you have new learning, knowledge and capability. To make the most of it here is an e-tivity to encourage you to consider your journey and offer encouragement to others.
Spark	Look back over the whole sequence of e-tivities and your own recordings in your e-portfolio and other postings, here or on social media. Revisit the e-moderator's summaries too and the plenary presentations from your group and others. Pick one key posting or comment you made that you feel represents something that you did not know, or perhaps fully understand, before the course began. Choose carefully.
1st individual contribution	Re-post your comment (maximum 100 words, so be selective or summarize) into the forum <link>, with an open source image that represents how you feel about learning it. Or take a photo for yourself. Post by <date>.
Dialogue begins	Take a look through the postings and images of others. Where you felt the same, tick 'like'; where you felt differently, tick '?' Against at least five of them, make a short, constructive and supportive suggestion on how your fellow participant might take his or her new knowledge forward. This might be another course of learning, further actions, sharing elsewhere, a note of a resource or direct offer of a meeting to discuss or anything else you can think of that may help them to apply their new knowledge in the future. Complete by <date>.
2nd individual contribution	Between <date and date> (allow two or three days maximum) undertake one posting, committing to actually doing something with the new knowledge you first mentioned.
Schedule and time	Takes about 2.5 hours in total over a week or so of calendar time. Works well as part of a series of revision e-tivities or where you are including reflections in final assignments.

Example E . . . continued

Numbering, pacing and sequencing	Put your e-tivity stage number and sequence number here.
Next	Create the future: you're ready!

This e-tivity is suitable for Stage 5. It works for almost any topic and for entirely online and blended programmes. The better you've established the group, the more productive and constructive the suggestions are, but it's worth a try whatever's gone before!

I've run this e-tivity using the VLE/LMS forums, but I've seen it work well on micro-blogs (e.g. Twitter) and on Facebook.

If you've encouraged recording of 'critical learning incidents' or reflections throughout, it's quicker for them to do. Make sure the feedback and e-moderator's summaries are readily accessible by this stage in the course—they are useful for those who find personal reflection difficult.

Resources for practitioners 6

E-tivity continuum

Differences between an online activity and an e-tivity: A continuum

	Traditional online activities	E-tivities (constructivist and collaborative)
		E-tivities for participative learning
Activities for self-study and self-assessment	Knowledge-testing	Knowledge-generating
	Backward-looking (checks understanding of materials already covered)	Forward-looking (invites participants to identify, evaluate or apply ideas contained in new sources)
	Focus on knowledge created by others, which participants should acquire	Focus on constructing, sharing, refining and appropriating knowledge
	Designed for summative or self-assessment	Designed for formative assessment, or as a scaffold for subsequent summative assessment
	Designed for self-study or independent learning	Designed for collaborative, interdependent learning: peer input key to learning
	Mapped against content	Mapped against one stage of the five-stage model and associated outcomes
	One activity may cover many points	One clear purpose per e-tivity
	Single iteration (task done = end of activity)	Multiple iterations: reflection and feedback are an integral part
	Simple, traditional, safe	Complex, innovative, risky
	One right answer	Several possible right answers
	Limited creative contribution	Potential for highly creative contributions
	Role of e-moderator not critical	Role of e-moderator essential
	Closed exercise or quiz	Open responses and feedback in multiple formats, e.g. text, images, audio and video via discussion boards, wikis, blogs, voice boards, group canvases, etc.

Thanks to Professor A. Armellini for his experience and contribution to this chart.

STRUCTURES

Resources for practitioners 7

E-tivity planning

Designing e-tivities is a creative task and might take a little more time than you think. Start here:

Start with the end in mind

What do you want to achieve by this online activity? What pedagogical problem or challenge are you solving? How will it add to the participants' learning? How will you assess or evaluate the e-tivity?

First things first!

How will you introduce and start the e-tivity off? What online 'sparks' do you have that will entertain? How much notice will the participants need? Can you think of a great title? If not, come back to it later.

Think win–win

Why will people want to take part? Will it add obvious and clear value to their learning? How will the group work together? How will you make it easy for everyone to contribute?

Sharpen the saw

How will you prepare yourself to make this e-tivity a success? Collect up your ideas and resources. What will the participants need to do to take part successfully? How will this e-tivity fit in the sequence?

Be proactive

Plan the e-moderator role and actions. How often will the e-moderator need to intervene? When will the e-moderator summarize and give feedback? What will you do about non-participation? Be realistic about the timings, but be prepared to adjust them if necessary.

Seek to understand

Try the e-tivity out on someone. What happens if the e-tivity doesn't go as you planned? How can you get information to change it for next time?

My spark for this resource is drawn from Steven Covey's seven habits of effective people and principle-centred leadership ideas (Covey, 2004).

Building programmes and processes with e-tivities

One, two, three or 30 e-tivities can be used within any kind of learning programme, blended with other methods, deployed across different technologies and techniques of teaching or combined with other online resources in a wide variety of ways. On a campus you can combine e-tivities with face-to-face lectures, lab work, classroom-based tutorials, creative events, practice and visits. The only limits are those of your own imagination and creativity. The best way to decide is to do a 'storyboard' first (see pages 191–3).

This resource offers three examples of putting a series of e-tivities together within the framework of the five-stage model.

Example 1 (20 e-tivities)

Example 1 shows an entirely online course with only the minimum of supplied resources, such as an e-book. Here, four e-tivities are offered each week and the cohort of participants is expected to finish the set of e-tivities at the end of each week and move on together to the next week. This is a popular and successful pattern.

Week	1	2	3	4	5	Total e-tivities
E-tivities 1–4 (Stage 1)	▓					4
E-tivities 5–8 (Stage 2)		▓				4
E-tivities 9–12 (Stage 3)			▓			4
E-tivities 13–16 (Stage 4)				▓		4
E-tivities 17–20 (Stage 5)					▓	4
(20 e-tivities)						

Example 2 (nine e-tivities)

Example 2 shows a more intensive course, where participants take part in short e-tivities for two weeks, experience face-to-face seminars and then go back online for further work and e-tivities, applying the ideas and reflecting on the learning. They are expected to offer around six hours online in the first two weeks, meet for seven hours and then go online for a further three. They then undertake around six hours of work to write up their experience.

Week	1	2	3	4	Total e-tivities
E-tivities 1–4 (Stage 1–3)	▓				4
E-tivities 5–8 (Stage 4)		▓			4
Face-to-face meeting			▒		0
E-tivity 9 (Stage 5)				▓	1
(9 e-tivities)					

Example 3 (twelve e-tivities)

Example 3 shows a course based on a twelve-week university or college semester, with a one-week 'catch-up' break two-thirds of the way through. Here most e-tivities last around two weeks, and the stages overlap each other. Participants need to commit around three hours per week online. This pattern could include a wide variety of other activities.

Week	1	2	3	4	5	6	7	8	9	10	11	12	Total e-tivities
E-tivities 1–2 (Stage 1)		▓											2
E-tivities 3–5 (Stage 2)			▓										3
E-tivities 6–7 (Stage 3)				▓	▓								2
E-tivities 8–10 (Stage 4)					▓	▓	▓	▓					2
E-tivities 11–13 (Stage 5)										▓	▓	▓	3
(12 e-tivities)													

Time estimates

By far the commonest, and maybe the most important question anyone ever asks me is 'How much time will creating and delivering e-tivities take?'. I present each of these issues in terms of quantities. You should be able to see how you can reduce or increase the amount of time by manipulating them.

Key factors

The stage of the model

- Typically at Stages 1 to 2 of the five-stage model, e-moderators do more, participants a little less, while the group is being established.
- At Stage 3, more structured tasks mean that participants do more, e-moderators do less (but this needs greater care).
- At Stage 4, the group is well established, and constant e-moderating presence is rarely needed. Good e-tivity structure and scheduling mean that participants can undertake some e-moderation and group leadership roles.
- At Stage 5, look for increasing independence by individuals and groups. A light touch from staff is usually appropriate.

The e-tivities

- Effective design and consequent interest in and contribution to the e-tivities by the participants.
- Participants' and e-moderator's emotional comfort with the online learning process.
- E-tivities and resources that can be reused.

Staff time

E-tivity designers

● Think out the e-tivity, explore it with others and plan it well in advance. Estimate: 1 hour (less if in a Carpe Diem process).
● If you plan to issue resources that are copyrighted, leave time to get permission. Avoid this if you can by using Open Educational Resources.
● Write, quality-check and put invitation messages in place online. Estimate: 1 hour first time, 0.5 hours second and subsequent times. Pilot by asking others to read instructions and respond: 0.5 hours. Less if working in a Carpe Diem process.
● Set up the bulletin board and resources: 1 hour first time, 0.5 hours after that.

E-moderating

● Respond to any e-mails and questions from participants or groups: 0.5 hours.
● Brief any team leaders (if necessary): 0.5 hours.
● E-moderate by weaving and feedback the e-tivity: 1 hour per week.
● Summarize and plenarize: extra 0.5 hours.
● Evaluation and feed-forward to next time: up to 0.5 hours.

Technical support

● Depends on platform and e-tivity designers experience but may need 0.5 hours for the first time.
● Provide technical support and help to participants as necessary: 1 hour if participants are inexperienced, much less at Stages 3 to 5.

Participant time

● Read invitation message, discuss online with other participants or e-moderator if necessary: 0.5 hours.
● Take part: up to 1.5 hours per week, more if fully collaborative.
● Explore, reflect and apply ideas, knowledge and understanding: 1 hour per week.
● Read and use summary: 0.5 hours.

Notes:
1. Very discursive e-tivities such as those sometimes used in social sciences or humanities courses may take longer for e-moderators and participants.
2. Designing e-tivities within Carpe Diem workshops (see Chapter 5) results in good e-tivities and less design time, with available technical support and feedback from participants.

Technical aspects

● Everyone's experience with the platform in use.
● Quality and appropriateness of platforms in use for the e-tivities.
● Levels and availability of good technical support in the early stages.
● Whether the technology is easily available at any time and from any place and/or good mobile apps available.
● Add some time in case the technology goes unexpectedly down.

Impact of success

- The numbers of participants.
- The levels of contribution expected and achieved.
- Levels of commitment and motivation from students, number of contributions, and amount of e-moderator time required to respond and summarize.
- Amount of browsing and vicarious learning. If more active participation is expected but not achieved due to weak e-tivity design, e-moderators can spend huge amounts of time trying to persuade some participants to contribute.

E-moderating

- Amount and effectiveness of e-moderator's training.
- E-moderator's flexibility and organizational skills.
- E-moderator's skills and experience in weaving and summarizing.
- E-moderator's cultural background and language skills.
- The number of other pressures on the e-moderator's time.
- The amount of the e-moderator's skill and experience in handling new constructs of online time.
- Amount of e-moderator knowledge of the topic and/or first time undertaken this participator unit or module.

At the lower levels of the five stages, participants need less time, e-moderators more. Further up the five-stage model, participants need more time, e-moderators less (except for summaries and plenaries).

When you have run an e-tivity once or twice, post an idea of how long it'll take participants in total and for the subsequent parts—they will appreciate this advice!

Resources for practitioners 10

Counting the delivery time

When designing your e-tivities it is most important to have a sense of how long both participants and e-moderators will need. Here are some tables to consider. The times that they give exclude designing and preparing the e-tivity and concentrate on the online time required from the moment that the first participant reads and responds to the e-tivity invitation.

These estimates are based on trained and experienced e-moderators and relatively straightforward and text-based e-tivities through bulletin boards or wikis. Using voice responses is generally a bit quicker for participants.

Novice e-moderators and participants will take longer to read and summarize; untrained e-moderators will take much longer. The length and complexity of messages also make a difference. For example, simpler and/or shorter messages can be expected from first-year undergraduates, compared with academics in a staff development programme.

Example 1

This is a simple e-tivity at Stages 1 or 2 with a group of 15 participants. The e-tivity requires participants to put in some information already known to them, and to respond to messages from others. These timings assume an efficient forum platform that is easy to navigate around and easy for posting messages.

E-tivity plan: Example 1

This simple e-tivity requires 56 mins from the participants.

Online action	Time spent	Number of messages	Number of minutes spent writing/posting	Read/view e-moderators
E-tivity 1: engage with a short spark and think	1	10		
Post message in response to e-tivity invitation			8	
On a later visit, read contributions of 15 others	15	20		
Post response to the contributions of others (respond to two other messages)			8	10
Totals	16 messages	30 mins	16 mins	10 mins

This e-moderator is fortunate that there is a quick summarizing function in her software platform to save time. He or she needs around 90 minutes.

Online action	Number of messages to read	Number of minutes spent reading	Number of minutes spent posting, archiving, summarizing and acknowledging
E-tivity 1: 15 initial postings plus 30 responses	45	45	
Quickly acknowledge each participant's initial response			15
Acknowledging further responses and summarizing			30
Totals	45 messages	45 mins	45 mins

As you can see, for the simplest of e-tivities, each participant will spend 56 minutes directly engaged in the e-tivity, spread over at least two visits. And for the e-moderator, the commitment is 85 minutes, probably in at least three visits.

Example 2

This e-tivity is at Stage 3 and involves a slightly more complicated process of three groups of five investigating a topic, followed by a group plenary with all 15 participants involved.

E-tivity plan: Example 2

Online action	Number of messages to read	Number of minutes spent reading and investigating the 'spark'	Number of minutes spent writing/posting
E-tivity 2, week 1: read e-tivity invitation and think	1	10	
Form into small groups, introductions and establish ways of working together	10	10	10
Undertake e-tivity in small groups, post output from small group into larger group plenary forum	20	20	30
Week 2, re-form in larger groups. Read summaries from small groups	3	10	
Whole groups discussion, compare and contrast	30	30	15
Read e-moderator summary, feedback and critique	1	15	
Totals	65 messages	95 mins	55 mins

Participants could spend nearly four hours on this e-tivity spread over two weeks.

Online action	Number of messages to read	Number of minutes spent reading	Number of minutes spent writing/posting
E-tivity 2, week 1: answer questions about process and requirements	10	10	10
Briefly look into small groups to ensure all are working	10	10	
Remind of posting times into whole-group plenary, and negotiate any extensions	5	5	20
Week 2, re-form in larger groups. Read summaries from small groups	3	9	
Whole-groups discussion, compare and contrast, occasionally post to keep on track	20	20	10
Summarize plenary discussion and post closing message	30	30	30
Totals	78 (some revisited to undertake summary)	84	70

For this e-tivity, the participants have spent roughly half of their time (95 minutes) reading messages; and a little less time posting their own responses. Much of the e-moderator's time is concentrated at the end of week 2, in reading and providing a good summary and evaluation of the final plenary.

After Stage 3, you can expect more reading and contribution time from participants, and more time for summarizing from e-moderators.

WRITING INVITATIONS

Resources for practitioners 11

Correspondence protocol

Most people are now familiar with online communication. However, it's worth exploring and reinforcing good styles and approaches, especially for e-tivities, where the action centres so much on exchange and contribution.

Good online communication cannot be directed. Simply posting codes of practice or protocols on websites doesn't really achieve much, since guidelines need to be grounded and applied to be meaningful.

You can use these lists as sparks in e-tivities, and ask participants to apply them, work on them and, especially, build on them or invent their own. You might also like to encourage discussion on whether, if you make rules, they can easily be applied and what you will do about transgression.

Message conventions

Use group conferencing, bulletin board or forum, blogs, wikis or most forms of social media when the message is intended for everyone in a particular group, such as in response to an e-tivity and when you expect that everyone will have the right to reply.

- Be aware of whether the message is available to a particular group through a password, through their 'following' or befriending you, through their knowledge of the URL or whether it is potentially open and searchable to the world.

- Choose a short, effective, enticing title for your message. We know titles are very important in enticing people to open the rest of the message. If there is no message line option (e.g. in Twitter), then use a hashtag that provides a link to similar topics.
- If you reply to someone and change the topic, change the title too.
- Whether you are the e-moderator or a participant, post your message in a way that suggests you invite a reply.
- If you are responding to someone else, then make it clear to what you are responding and to whom.
- If you reply to just one part of someone else's message, copy and paste their words into the start of your e-mail, so it's clear which sections you are referring to.
- Be prepared to describe how you feel as well as what you think.
- Avoid putting words into capital letters—they are considered to be equivalent to shouting.
- Ensure that you place new messages in the *appropriate* place. When designing e-tivities, make sure a place for response is prepared before participants' arrival, so the right place to respond and engage is clear.
- Keep to one topic per message, with a relevant title. It's far better to send several short messages with different titles than one long one covering many subjects.
- If you need to make a number of points in a message, label them 1, 2, 3. This way it is easy for others to respond.
- If you are making a link, test that your recipients will be able to open and view it.
- If you are attaching a document, make sure the title is clear and there are one or two lines of description in the message so that your recipients can decide whether, and how soon, they need to download the document.

Use your 'announcements' blog:

- Convey information or instructions that should or must be seen by the whole group.

When and how to use e-mail:

- Use e-mail to message one or several specific people.

- Address messages directly to people who need to take action and/or reply to you. You can copy people into e-mail messages if you believe they need to know about the content, but avoid including people unnecessarily. If e-mails are 'copied' rather than sent 'to' people, it's reasonable for them to assume the message is for information and that they need not take action.
- *Never forward an e-mail you have received on to someone without permission of the originator.* Similarly be careful about a long e-mail stream being attached inadvertently and possibly inappropriately.
- You can build groups of people to e-mail for your convenience. Use these cautiously and only when your message concerns everyone in that group. Using a forum, blog or wiki might be better.
- If you receive a message that has been addressed to a number of people, think carefully before replying to all of them. You might only need to make the comment to the originator of the message, or one or two other people. Some people get *very annoyed* about many minor e-mails circulating around large groups.
- If you receive a message that contains a 'reply all' to a large group including you, and which you consider irrelevant, simply delete it. Avoid replying to 'all' again in your anger and perpetuating the problem.
- Avoid setting up automatic replies to messages if you are away, unless really necessary. Try, instead, to pick them up from wherever you are.

Resources for practitioners 12

Learning 'Netspeak'

I've used the term 'Netspeak' in this book for the kind of action-based communications I've tried to harness. This term comes from David Crystal's books about new types of language (Crystal, 2004, 2008).

Talking online, sometimes called 'Netspeak', lacks the facial expressions, gestures and conventions that can be important in communicating face-to-face and in conveying personal opinions and attitudes. In most online platforms, participants and e-moderators alike must always be alert to the potential for ambiguity. This phenomenon led to the development of 'smileys' or 'emoticons' as a substitute. Incidentally, the word 'emoticon' is derived from the term 'emote', as a means to indicate a virtual *action* (Crystal, 2004).

There is little point in simply telling e-moderators and participants about Netspeak. Design a little e-tivity so they can understand and practise! Here are some ideas to try. E-tivities around these ideas are ideal for Stages 1 and 2 and where you are using a mainly text-based platform (e.g. bulletin boards, wikis, blogs, etc.).

- *Netspeak* uses < > to indicate an *action*, such as a giggle or a look. Get everyone to show an action in their own networds. Abbreviations for actions are fine if everyone understands them: for example, <g> for grin. It would be a good idea to explain new networds at least for the first two or three times you use them.

- *Capitals* are considered shouting. Invent other means of emphasis and see if they help with meaning.
- *Brevity* is all-important, mainly because of the length of time it takes both to type and then to read text on a screen. Try putting up sentences of different lengths and encouraging discussion on their effect. Start a discussion on the value or otherwise of restricting characters, such as when micro-blogging (e.g. Twitter).
- Contributions should clearly relate to the *purpose of the exchange*. Always define purposes and constantly remind people about them. Be prepared to set up new areas for discussion if fresh issues come up, but make their purpose clear, too.
- *Me too*. Much electronic communication is about people making their mark rather than adding a contribution as such. Set up an e-tivity to enable them to announce their arrival. Look for features in the software that help with saying 'me too'.

David Crystal's books are great for understanding the English language in a variety of contexts, including online. You might like to try one of his YouTube videos as a spark for your e-tivities.

Resources for Practitioners 1 from page 97 offers more ideas.

DEVELOPMENT AND IMPROVEMENT

Resources for practitioners 13

Building motivating e-tivities

- Does the e-tivity need 'chunking up' into small pieces to be more motivating? (The answer is usually yes!)
- Can participants cope with it all in one go? (Smaller chunks are better.)
- What is the extrinsic reward of taking part? Make this clear throughout each and every e-tivity.
- Are the intentions of the e-tivity clear? Do participants know exactly what's expected of them and why?
- Who will find this e-tivity easy? How can you stretch them?
- Who will find this e-tivity hard? How can you support them?
- Is the e-tivity at the right level for the group—will everyone see it as worthwhile?
- Is the e-tivity at the right stage of the five-stage model, i.e. addressing what the group is likely to benefit from?
- Who will the participants want to please by taking part? Can you build this into the e-tivity?
- Are there cultural aspects that might alienate, confuse and hence demotivate some participants? How can you turn these into positive benefits?
- Is the layout of the e-tivity invitation clear? Have you proofed the message before posting it?
- What will participants lose by *not* taking part? Or by merely lurking?

- Is the spark engaging?
- At Stages 1 and 2, do not expect intrinsic motivation to help. Be clear about the benefits, the purpose and reason for participating in the e-tivities. What do participants get out of it? For example, does it contribute to an up-and-coming assessment?
- At Stages 4 and 5, try to promote intrinsic motivators.
- Avoid 'punishment' and threats to non-participants or forced attempts at achieving contribution through assessment—they do not motivate.
- Fabulous technology and comfort with the system will only ever be a hygiene factor, not a motivator in itself.

Resources for practitioners 14

Online emotions

There are many factors involved in the personal abilities that contribute to learning and achieving. One major aspect is known as emotional quotient (EQ) (Goleman, 2011). Emotions and more unconscious aspects of learning need to be given time to develop. It is worthwhile trying to promote an increase in EQ in your participants through your five-stage scaffold and your e-tivities, as the online groups will achieve more, and more comfortably.

Working online creates a wide range of feelings in participants and in e-moderators. Frustration with the technology is common but this is often soon forgotten. The experience of not physically being with others in the same space is probably the main emotional trigger. Isolation has two dimensions. One is distance in place (being alone) and the other is psychological (distance in thoughts, feeling alone).

Features of high EQ include:

- self-awareness;
- management of the emotions;
- self-motivation;
- the ability to read the emotions of others;
- handling relationships (without being subsumed by them)—for example, making personal connections, being good at defusing explosive situations;
- taking time for reflection.

Here are some ideas for e-tivity design and e-moderation:

- Set up simple rules at the beginning to take care of 'feelings'. These can include always acknowledging feelings and offering support.
- Base the design of group processes on principles that take account of holistic emotional needs, not just given learning objectives.
- If things go particularly well or badly, draw the group's attention immediately to the reasons—the consequences of actions.
- Train your e-moderators to keep all online responses in polite and measured tones to avoid inflaming feelings unnecessarily.
- Train your e-moderators to systematize their responses to common online emotional issues, and enable them to practise through being online learners themselves.

Working with online emotions

Online, emotions may be expressed in different ways. Some are explicit and some are more subtle. With the advent of gesture-based computing and avatars in virtual worlds, some emotions can be conveyed through 'body' movements —such as clapping, nodding and so on. Using voice is also an excellent idea too, since tone and inflections add emotional value to a message. There are good voice boards or easy ways of using podcasts (Salmon and Edirisingha, 2008) available, such as Wimba, to help you.

But you might mainly be using text. Here are some for examples:

Emoticons

Emoticon	Meaning
:-)	Happy
:-D	Very happy/laughing
;-)	Wink
:-P ;-P	Poking tongue out/wink
:-(	Sad
:'-) :'-(	Tear: happy/sad
:-O	Surprise/shock/yawn
:-/	Sceptical/undecided/not sure

Describe the emotion in words

- I felt uncomfortable when . . .
- I just can't believe I was offline when you replied so quickly to my news.
- When I read about your achievement, I felt I had to congratulate you.
- I was sad to hear that . . . It reminded me of when I . . .

Describe your body language

- When I read your message, I jumped for joy!
- Laughing so hard I nearly fell off my chair . . .!
- I smiled when I read about . . .
- Ha ha, I said out loud!
- Mmmmm . . . walking about wondering about that . . .

Developing attunement to text-expressed emotions

- Lots of punctuation marks!!!!!!, CAPITAL LETTERS or short sentences suggest a rapid and possibly angry response.
- Sentences that start by denying a feeling, such as 'I'm not sexist but . . .' or 'I'm not easily upset but . . .' sometimes mean the opposite.
- A direct challenge in the form of a question (rather different from exploratory questions)—for example, 'Didn't you promise that . . .?' or 'Haven't you heard the research that proves . . .?'—may suggest irritation.
- Some people become annoyed and distracted by typos and spelling mistakes in messages, especially if they are unused to online communication, and express indignation. E-moderators should convey to participants that the occasional spelling or grammatical error in e-tivities is acceptable— participation is what counts.

Emotions can be expressed through

- short messages, suggesting a prompt response, indicative of a sense of excitement and shared joy;
- use of words or phrases with single exclamation marks both in message titles and in the body of the message, for example, 'brilliant!', 'wham!', 'fab news!', 'congratulations!';
- references to actions and body language, such as 'jumped for joy', 'clapped my hands';

- using narrative voice, or use of an asterisk, i.e., * or third person references to yourself to indicate you are describing actions you are currently feeling in order to create more real-world interactions, such as 'sigh . . .', 'Michael ponders . . .', *shrugs*, *shakes head*, *blushing*, *scuffing foot in dirt in embarrassment*;
- references to ongoing relationship and interest, for example, 'interested in your findings', 'can I help?';
- careful use of words, often describing body language, such as 'fantastic news, well done', 'when I read your email I gave such a yahoo!';
- being more 'economical', or humourous, such as 'I've just read your e-mail about the research grant. Congratulations! Well done!' or 'I wish I had an unsend button. I do value your contribution to this project and hope that you accept my apology and that we can get back to the good working relationship we had.'

Some words for expressing emotions

special	wow	congratulations
well done	great	fantastic
reward	hard work	tell me more
celebrate	thrilled	significant
recognize		

Negative emotions can be expressed by use of exclamations, emoticons and apologies (from sincere to downright grovelling).

Key strategies for defusing negative emotions

- 'I could be entirely wrong—it has been known!';
- Apology combined with self-deprecation;
- Apology combined with question—rhetorical or otherwise;
- Positive compliment and/or sentiment about continued positive relationship;
- Fairly blunt affirmation and use of negative feelings to reinforce the message.

Resources for practitioners 15

More intelligent e-tivities

As you get into the swing of developing and running e-tivities, you may want to start to look at them more creatively. But try to avoid making them longer! Instead, start to think of putting the pieces together. This is one way to view the term 'intelligence': to mean the use of wisdom, insight, intuition and experience (MacGilchrist, Myers and Reed, 2004) I've borrowed from MacGilchrist *et al.*'s ideas in *The Intelligent School* for the list that follows.

Here are some ideas to stimulate your thinking about e-tivities:

Contextual intelligence   Think about your e-tivities in relation to your wider community, your discipline, your department, your school, your learning outcomes and your latest research. What is really important in these areas? Use the key issue as a spark. Adapt your e-tivities as new theories and ideas arise.

Strategic intelligence   Scan the literature for what's coming up and what might be important in the future, and use these ideas as goals and purposes for e-tivities. Create and convey vision and promote forward thinking in your participants.

Academic intelligence   Put high value on the scholarship of ideas that arise out of your e-tivities and achievements, especially group outcomes. Recognize and celebrate the effective learning that emerges. Especially highlight true engagement with a topic and with the construction of knowledge. Strongly encourage the sharing of academic insights.

Reflective intelligence   Build continually on the core skills and processes of monitoring, reflecting upon and evaluating every e-tivity. Look for knowledge that can be shared and built upon further.

Pedagogical intelligence   You will have realized by now that developing expertise in online pedagogy is what e-tivities are all about. Pedagogical intelligence refers to the complex and dynamic relationship between teaching and learning and is a key issue in the quality of e-tivities, ensuring that they are 'fit for purpose'. They need to be tried out, evaluated and constantly adjusted for this form of intelligence to flourish.

Collegial intelligence   In the spirit of the widely shared knowledge, make sure that staff and students work together to improve good practice in your e-tivities. Share ideas within disciplines and across them. Reflect constantly to improve e-tivity design and increase your confidence and comfort with e-moderating and with virtual groups.

Emotional intelligence   Allow the feelings of everyone involved in e-tivities to surface, be owned, expressed and respected. This is especially important with computer-mediated learning, where the technology itself may generate a wide range of positive and negative feelings. Try to foster opportunities for promoting interpersonal intelligence in your e-tivities through encouraging participants to appreciate a wide variety of points of view. Encourage intra-personal intelligence through forming and developing models of understanding.

Spiritual intelligence   Spiritual intelligence means tapping into the lives and development of each participant in an e-tivity in a way that will not necessarily be very tangible or measurable. This is the 'X' factor in e-tivities—a compassion that can be conveyed through online mediation. Create space to reflect on big issues. Watch out for their happening by chance—and foster any that you can.

Ethical intelligence   Recognize and value the rights of all participants in e-tivities and foster the surfacing of the beliefs and values that underlie the online processes. Promote equality of access to the e-tivity opportunities that open up through a wide variety of technologies and motivation. E-moderate for equality and learning opportunities.

Disabilities and e-tivities

Because of their simplicity, e-tivities offer online group learning to participants with disabilities that might hinder their capacity to take part in more conventional learning activities. In most countries, legislation requires at least minimum access to courseware for disabled learners. E-tivities help, as they can be based on clear invitational messages and enable all contributions to be equally valued.

Online, disabilities and special needs are rarely obvious unless the participant chooses to write about them. People with speech or hearing difficulties are not at any disadvantage in text-based messaging.

Technology can help or hinder, of course. Keyboard or speech commands can be provided for those unable to use a mouse. Electronic text can be designed so that it converts to Braille. With forethought, Web and LMS/VLE pages can be designed to be more effective for certain disabilities, although the increased emphasis on graphics has created new challenges. In constructing e-tivities, consider the font and style and how e-tivity invitations might look on a variety of screens and to different people. This will help those with partial visual impairment, but will also be of benefit to all participants.

There is a range of helpful instructional literature on the topic of online design for disability considerations (Coombs, 2010), and a multitude of technology services available that can support designing learning for special education needs. Resources such as *iPhone, iPad and iPod Touch Apps for (Special) Education* (Sailers, 2009) or *Apps for Special Education* (Spectronics, 2012) can provide e-tivity designers with a rundown of applications available and examples of how to use them in learning design.

Mobility

Learning online can be an open door for those with restricted mobility or difficulty in accessing buildings. E-tivities provide opportunities to 'travel', meet and learn with others with comparative ease, if accessible materials and processes are on offer.

Participants who have problems with their vision or physical movement might find that the keyboard and screen prevent them from contributing as much as they would like, or as quickly as others. For example, those who cannot freely move their hands and arms may not use the keyboard at a reasonable speed and may need special equipment or speech recognition software. However, the short bursts of activity required by e-tivities, and the emphasis on contribution rather than reading, often help with attention and mobility problems.

Dyslexia

Participants with learning difficulties, such as dyslexia, often find that they can contribute better through their keyboards, and through asynchronous bulletin boards, wikis and forums, than they can in synchronous chat rooms or face-to-face meetings. They have an opportunity to rearrange their words and sentences before committing them to the rest of the group. However, they will have more difficulty if the platform does not offer a spell-checker for all their text. They can prepare messages in a word processor, spell-check and then upload, but this may slow their responses. Everyone, however, needs to be reassured that mistakes in typing or spelling are not important with e-tivities. It's the thought or contribution that counts! The odd spelling or grammatical error should worry nobody.

Vision

Blind participants cannot use a mouse so need to become adept at keyboard commands. They can adapt software through Braille printouts of messages or through using speech synthesis. An experienced intermediary is needed to train and support blind users to the point of competence and independence. When changes are made to the system, blind participants must be notified early so that they can arrange in advance for specific adaptations and training.

Blind users frequently develop good keyboard skills for inputting. In an emergency they can have short e-tivities read to them.

PARTICIPANTS' EXPERIENCE

Resources for practitioners 17

Contributions

You might find my nine categories for analysing contributions to e-tivities helpful. They work best in discussion-type forums or where there is an online plenary following an e-tivity. The analytical categories make it easier to see what is happening in the debate.

If you wish to assess for contribution, they provide a framework.

Individual thinking

1 Offering up ideas or resources and inviting a critique of them.
2 Asking challenging questions.
3 Articulating, explaining and supporting positions on issues.
4 Exploring and supporting issues by adding explanations and examples.
5 Reflecting on and re-evaluating personal opinions.

Interactive thinking

6 Offering a critique, challenging, discussing and expanding ideas of others.
7 Negotiating interpretations, definitions and meanings.
8 Summarizing and modelling previous contributions.
9 Proposing actions based on ideas that have been developed.

Resources for practitioners 18

Patterns of participation

Each individual participant develops his or her own pattern of logging on and taking part in a series of e-tivities. Here are some of the most common patterns and some ideas on how the e-moderator can help them.

Patterns of participation

Type	Behaviours	E-moderator response
The wolf	Visits once a week, lots of activity, then disappears again until next week, or even the week after!	Nudge wolf by e-mail to encourage to visit again and see responses that he or she has sparked off. Point to e-tivity that might interest wolf.
The elephant	Steady—visits most days for a short time.	Congratulate. Ask elephant to encourage and support others—especially mouse and squirrel.
The squirrel	Always catching up: completes two weeks in one session then disappears again for some time.	Nudge squirrel by e-mail to suggest life is easier with more regular access. Check on other commitments. Provide regular summaries and archiving to enable squirrel to catch up easily and contribute.
The mouse	Visits once a week, reads and contributes little.	Check that mouse can access all messages. Check language difficulties. May need boost of confidence. Give specific role.
The mole	Inclined to post disembodied comments in a random way.	Try to include relevant comments from mole in summaries and invite responses. Needs support and 'e-stroking'.
The rabbit	Lives online, prolific message writer, responds very rapidly.	Rabbit may need counselling to hold back and let others shine through. Give structured roles such as summarizing after a plenary.
The stag	Tendency to dominate discussion at certain times.	Invite stag back frequently. Offer a structured and specific role.
The magpie	Steals ideas without acknowledging.	Foster a spirit of acknowledgement and reinforcement of individual ideas. Warn magpie directly if necessary.
The dolphin	Intelligent, good communicator and playful online. May annoy participants who think it's all very serious.	Ensure dolphin acknowledges and works well with others.

Resources for practitioners 19

Flow and e-tivities

As you gain experience and confidence in creating your e-tivities, you might also be a little more ambitious. At this point, some e-tivity designers tend to rush off for more multi-media content, or a better platform, or larger numbers. Of course, those ideas may be very valuable. However, adding a little more 'magic' to your e-tivities might also be worth trying, especially as participants become experienced and enthusiastic in working online, and the role of the technology becomes less important.

As a spark, you could consider the concept of autotelism. Autotelic theories derive from Csikszentmihalyi's (2002) studies of enjoyment and the conditions that underlie it. Autotelism originally described creative processes such as making music, or more physical activities such as sports. Csikszentmihalyi researched creating 'flow'—which derives from unconscious value deriving from the experience itself. Flow suggests a state that generates pleasure, gratification and intrinsic motivation for the participant. We are familiar with how this works in a successful face-to-face group—we sense the 'buzz' and participants often tell us how much they *enjoyed* taking part.

Researchers applied these ideas to computing (Ghani and Deshpande, 1994) and to teaching and learning (Lawrence and Gammon, 2004). Online, the aim is that participants become similarly immersed in the experience and forget about problems (such as the technology). They lose 'self-consciousness' and feel part of the ongoing online group or community.

There has been some work that has investigated the theory of flow (or optimum experience) and its effect on students' attitudes and experiences by using 3-D immersive worlds (Forte, Gomes, Gondim and de Almeida, 2011; Yu-Chih, Backman and Backman, 2010). Results confirmed that creating a sense of enjoyment contributed to positive and successful learning experiences and attitudes towards engaging with online learning. You can read more about virtual worlds and e-tivities in *E-moderating* (Salmon, 2011).

These are my suggestions for the seven conditions for autotelic e-tivities.

Challenging activities that require skill The best e-tivities are those that are stretching, worthwhile and active. They need to generate a sense of mastery and engagement in the participants. Think carefully about challenging outcomes for your e-tivities, but allow sufficient time for participants to be successful, and don't make your invitations too complicated.

Merging of awareness and action You will observe that some participants in e-tivities become deeply involved in the online action and interaction—others less so. Try to encourage those who do become involved to partner those who are less enthusiastic for appropriate support.

Clear goals and feedback After you have run an e-tivity a few times, you will know what works and be able to offer clearer goals and more effective feedback on achievement by participants. Encourage them to create their own goals and feedback, too.

Concentration on the task in hand Make the task as relevant as possible and promote the interaction. Check back constantly with participants how they are feeling (not just how they are thinking!). The idea of authentic and useful tasks will help here. Ensure that the group is well socialized and integrated at Stage 2 before moving on to Stage 3.

Paradox of control This is a complicated concept but one that I think applies well to online learning. What participants need most is not a sense of being in control, but of exercising control in difficult circumstances and of moving away from safe routines. The scaffolding of the five-stage model allows for this increasing sense of mastery. So it is important to ensure that e-tivities continue to be stretching and appropriate as the participants move up through the stages, and that participants are gradually encouraged to be more self-determined. Try to make e-tivities interesting and worthwhile in themselves, diverting participants away from constant attention to assessment.

Loss of self-consciousness Autotelism suggests that when we cease to be self-focused we have a chance to expand our ideas of who we are. Working online in diverse groups promotes self-reflection and widens understandings. It is therefore worthwhile designing e-tivities that explore expanding concepts of identity, such as using creative techniques or borrowing ideas from other disciplines. Such e-tivities can easily be offered from Stage 2 onwards. Resources for Practitioners 1 and 2 on pages 97–128 offer many ideas.

Transformation of time One of the commonest aspects of autotelism is a different experience of time passing compared to clock watching! Csikszentmihalyi suggests 'freedom from the tyranny of time'. We know that online time takes on a quite different construct. Sometimes, people are amazed how long they have been online because they have been so involved. At Stages 4 and 5 of the model, we should encourage participants to 'go with the flow of time' and take what time they need, and can, to benefit most from the experience.

Resources for practitioners 20

E-tivity feedback and plenaries

The better you design your e-tivities, the less e-moderator intervention is needed. However, even with a great design and scaffolding, the more skill the e-moderator has, the more the participants feel that there is supportive and valuable presence from the e-moderator.

There's much more about e-moderating in my 2011 book (Salmon, 2011), but if you want to get started immediately the key skills are *weaving* and *summarizing*.

Weaving

Weaving is used to keep an e-tivity or a discussion going forward. Weaving is the key way of *adding value* from the teacher or tutor as well as promoting and encouraging further work on the topic. You may wish to blend the weave within different formats such as images and text.

The e-moderator can:

- offer feedback to highlight issue he or she thinks are important points;
- correct misunderstandings and explain something where needed;
- combine issues that may not be obvious to those taking part;
- give examples and illustrations to bring topics further to life;
- promote and encourage depth of understanding;
- collect up and 'tag' important issues.

Summarizing

Summarizing brings an e-tivity to a close, and provides a marker for moving onto the next. Some e-tivity summaries, outputs or outcomes can often most usefully be used as a spark for the next e-tivity in a sequence. A summary pulls together the main points. The e-moderator can then offer feedback or commentary of his or her own. Ideally, summarizing should note the main contributors to the e-tivity.

If you wish, participants can also usefully acquire and contribute the skills of summarizing. Or the role of summarizing can be taken by two or three people working collaboratively. Whoever undertakes the summary should always invite comment, by the original contributors, on its sufficiency and interpretation.

Summarizing is a succinct way to collate participants' responses to the e-tivities. As they move further into the learning scaffold and their ability to work together, the impact on knowledge construction and acquisition can often be tracked through the summaries.

Post the summary clearly on the platform, with a good title, so that it's easily accessed by latecomers or for revision.

Thanks to Professor Janet Gregory at Swinburne University of Technology for her contribution to this resource.

CARPE DIEM

Resources for practitioners 21

The Carpe Diem process

Designing together for active and interactive learning with e-tivities

Here is an overview of the whole Carpe Diem process, if you'd like to try one for yourselves. There's some detail about getting ready, and the activities to be carried out over the two days of the Carpe Diem workshop and afterwards.

My original ideas (which I'm not going to let go of in a hurry) were that we need to get together, design together and then deliver many times for the benefit of more participative, active and engaged learning. And we need to do it as quickly and efficiently as possible. Essentially it's still education, but not as we knew it in the past . . . Stand by—we are reshuffling the deck. Mobilize your creativity, suspend judgement, keep moving and just try this . . .

Get ready

1 First identify your module, unit or programme to be transformed. It can be a course where you want to change the mode of learning for any reason, or a new course. Make sure you've got your learning outcomes agreed

before you go into the Carpe Diem process. Try to keep your thinking as fluid as possible apart from that (for now).

2　Then identify your Carpe Diem workshop facilitator (see pages 197–8 for the suggested skills required).

3　Now build your Carpe Diem team, making sure they are available for the two-day workshop.

You will need:

- learning designer(s): people who understand the five-stage model and e-tivities;
- learning technologist(s): people to help you make the most of the technology platform(s) you have available;
- a librarian or a relevant information specialist: at least one. Ideally someone who can help you find legal, safe and free resources for your programme (but also see pages 125–8);
- a primary knowledge team: academics and/or teachers;
- 'reality checker(s)': peers, colleagues or students (for an hour or two on day 2).

Also, if possible:

- one of the team trained and/or experienced in Carpe Diem facilitation with understanding of the five-stage model and e-tivities process;
- one or more with some 'right-brain thinking', knowledge of creativity techniques, good at diagramming and/or the processes of innovation;
- one 'completer/finisher' to take responsibility for ensuring the action plan is viable and delivered.

Space and equipment needed

For day 1

You will need a collaborative space, whiteboards or flip charts, lots of brightly coloured sticky notes and pens. A poster or printout of the five-stage model and/or the five-stage pictures (they are in colour on the website www. e-tivities.com). Sustenance—food, water coffee. Avoidance of interruption. All the creativity everyone can muster. A nice big clock.

For day 2

You will need:

- networked computers;
- access to any prepared course sites, such as in your VLE/LMS, Facebook or whatever you are choosing to use;
- access to shared repositories for content if your institution has one;
- access to open educational resources repositories for your discipline.

Pre-Carpe Diem meeting

Two to four weeks before the Carpe Diem workshop, have your pre-meeting. Try to cover the following:

1   Introductions for everyone.
2   Check what individuals expect to get out of taking part and what they can contribute.
3   Explain what Carpe Diem offers, and how it works.
4   Explain timescales and commitments (see Resources for Practitioners 23).
5   Lead discussion on the unit/module/course/programme to be (re-)designed. Try to turn discussion around to the threshold knowledge that must be tackled and what pedagogical challenges they have that could be addressed through learning technologies. Gently introduce the idea that assessment on the course could be digitalized, if it's not already. Don't come up with solutions yet but get them all thinking about it.
6   Clarify what participants are willing to commit to undertaking, e.g. online e-moderation course, practise online e-tivities, give book or briefing about the five-stage model, an understanding about open educational resources (OERs), or an audit of resources. If they are unwilling or unable to do anything, get them to turn up for the Carpe Diem anyway.

The two-day Carpe Diem workshop process

We find it's best to run this over two consecutive days if you can. If not, of course there can be gaps in between the days—but make sure you keep all the resources and outputs from day 1 for day 2. We find it's quickest if all the Carpe Diem participants are co-located. Of course, you don't have to be in the same location but make sure your technology is good and stable if some people are remote—and you'll need good visual displays.

Summary of the stages

Day 1

1 Write a blueprint

Here you work together to lay out the essential aspects of what you aim to achieve.

Your output will be an agreed 'mission statement' for the course and some key choices on how the course will 'look and feel' online. You should move on when you feel confident that you've got reasonable agreement between the team on these.

2 Make a storyboard

Here you draw out the process of your learning, teaching and assessment in a visual way, working out your schedule, a sense of flow and alignment between the components. Use the five-stage model as a rough scaffold and your calendar for the delivery of the learning to participants to help you plan. Allow plenty of time to do this—but try to finish it by the end of day 1 if you can. Take it home, don't lose it. Put it under your bed for the night. You can review it quickly at the beginning of day 2, after 'sleeping on it'. It's your plan for transformation and impact.

Day 2

3 Build your prototype online

Now you try out your design in the online environment, and create some real e-tivities. Try to build at least six good, if draft, e-tivities—just use the invitation template and explanations on pages 2–3.

4 Check reality

Your designs are tried out by your reality checkers, to see how they work. Let them have a go and then listen carefully to their feedback. Try not to be too defensive. All feedback is valuable.

5 Review and adjust

Preview the work so far, make adjustments, refine timings, flag places to return to, indicate what additional work is needed and who should be responsible for it. You are ready to do the action plan when you can see a way from the storyboard and prototypes to a design vision of your online or blended course.

6 Planning your next steps

Now the team is ready to build an action plan together.

Some exercises to help you through the process

Day 1

Stage 1: Write a blueprint

Our mission is . . .

Agree on the overarching aims and intentions of your unit. Write a statement that captures those aims and intentions on the flip chart. You'll probably want to look carefully at your learning outcomes. If you find they are not perfect, then you can discuss them—but not for too long, please.

The 'look and feel' of our online unit . . .

Choose the adjectives that best describe the look and feel you would like for your unit, course or programme. Think what would you would like participants to say about their learning experience after it is complete. You may want to add some adjectives of your own. Can you *agree* on three or four of them?

textured, classy, trendy	postmodern	elite
professional	controversial	participative
simple	pleasant	eye-catching
bright	fun	accessible
relevant	daring	playful
compact	decisive	creative
smart	energetic	light
efficient	flashy	modern
fiery	basic	current
strong	blended	incisive
challenging	dynamic	mobile
engaging	demanding	global
reflective	edgy	enabling
clear	enticing	bland
contextualized	can-do	forward-looking
grand	unusual	flexible
managerial	purposeful	pacey
provocative		

Start at the end

'Begin with the end in mind' is number two of *Seven Habits of Highly Effective People* (Covey, 2004).

The focus now is how you are going to assess the impact from your e-tivities. Starting with the end in mind, before you plan your online learning programme, means that you get a very strong handle on what you are designing to achieve, the directions you need to take and the destination. You may find that you need to revisit your learning outcomes or your mission again.

Assessment can be contentious (especially for academics), but do your best to think differently about it. It's my experience that if you start creatively with assessment, designing uncommon, non-traditional approaches for learning come a little easier.

The idea here is to come up with a first shot at these questions:

- What *must* be assessed from your learning outcomes?
- What can be taught but not assessed?
- What offers opportunities for formative assessment and teaching feedback?
- How can you encourage peer feedback through e-tivities?
- What technologies will help you make assessment fairer, faster, cheaper?
- Consider aligning digital assessment with your new digital-driven e-tivities.

If your Carpe Diem team is naturally collaborative, you might be able to get some viable answers to these questions by discussion. If things get a bit stressy (they seem to with assessment!), try some fun, creative approaches—anything from brainstorming, reversal, provocation. Google 'creative techniques' if you need some ideas.

Stage 2: Make a storyboard

All the resources that you now have around you form a blueprint (your mission, the look and feel of your course, your decisions on assessments), but you need to create a process of integration and flow. I suggest you do this by 'storyboarding'.

Storyboarding means visually representing a process that you can later build. It needs to have something of the climate, what the key players do, how they move through the process, what the critical moments are in the 'story', and of course what it's all leading to and what happens in the end. If you are good at drawing, try a comic strip approach—look at some of the great storyboarding videos on YouTube. The sketches for the five-stage model on pages 19–33 and this book's website (www.e-tivities.com) demonstrate another way of visually building a story.

However, within the Carpe Diem workshop you'll probably want to start with a an easy collaborative way to do it. So try this:

How to do a storyboard with paper-based resources

1 Get the calendar for the delivery of your course and represent it on a whiteboard or (large) piece of pinned-up flip-chart paper. Draw a grid and create a column for each week that the course will run. You might need a week 'zero' too.

2 Divide what you must 'teach'/convey/cover into a series of discrete topics. It is usually best to start with one per week. Write each topic clearly onto a coloured sticky note—we usually use bright pink. Add these on the next row down on the grid, under the dates and week numbers.

3 Use a different coloured sticky note to represent assessment (say, bright yellow). If assessment only occurs at the end of the module, you should just have a single yellow sticky with a description of this, at the end of the storyboard. If assessment instances occur during the module, use yellow sticky notes throughout to represent them. Place them roughly where you think they might be needed in the calendar. On the storyboard make a note on the sticky notes of your first ideas as to what format of assessment you might use—for example, exam, presentation, multiple-choice questions, group presentation, etc. Don't forget to include key places for formative assessment and key forms of feedback, too.

4 Rewrite and move around the sticky notes until you are satisfied that as a first draft so far it looks viable.

5 Have a cup of tea.

6 Now, on the next line down on the grid, put your first idea for e-tivities appropriate to each section. Use a third-colour sticky note (say, green). Use one green sticky note for each e-tivity you identify. Paste these notes in the appropriate section of the board (it should start looking a bit like a storyboard now). On each green sticky note, at this stage, simply write the *purpose* of each e-tivity. You can have more than one in each week, or you can have e-tivities that span a couple of weeks.

7 If you are blending with face-to-face meetings, add in a sticky note (another colour) where your campus-based meetings, face-to-face tutorial work, use of a lab, site visits and so on will- or must-happen.

8 As ideas come, note them on the sticky notes; for example, what technologies, what are great OERs, who could help, etc. Don't argue about them yet—just place them somewhere for now.

9 Get the whole Carpe Diem team to stand up and group around the storyboard. Try to imagine what it would be like to be a participant taking part. 'Walk through' the process together. Make changes. Photograph version one. You'll change it later.

10 Move the green sticky notes around so that you have them roughly where you think they might ultimately happen. Start to write the numbering sequence on each green sticky notes—for example, 1.3 is first week, being the third e-tivity in sequence; 4.2 is the fourth week, being the second e-tivity in sequence.

11 Take another break. It's probably the end of day 1 anyway.

Options of working together for storyboarding

My experience is if you can get everyone together in a co-located way you can storyboard successfully, quickly . . . an easy transformation . . . that's the spirit of Carpe Diem! There's great joy in this kind of storyboard. For many people, storyboards are a true lightbulb moment and they can see why e-tivities need to be designed how they are. The scaffolding comes to life too.

Of course, it can be done in other ways! If you are co-located, use an electronic touch-table or some form of mapping software (see pages 67–8). If you are not physically in the same space, try anything from Skype or virtual classrooms (who is going to be first with a Second Life Carpe Diem?). Check out Chapter 4 for many more ideas for working with remote groups—it's not just for students, Carpe Diem participants and e-tivity designers can do it too.

Have you got through Stages 1 and 2 of Carpe Diem by the end of day 1?

If *not*, you've either not really gotten into the spirit of designing differently *or* you were hugely creative, fast and innovative from the start. Just take a minute or two before you move on to Stage 3 of Carpe Diem to decide which. Admire and review your storyboard from Day 1. And then. . .

Day 2

Stage 3: Build your prototypes online

1 Make sure everyone has a copy of what the invitation looks like and the advice on pages 2–3. It's good if they have some experience of e-tivity

design, but not essential. Everyone moves on and everyone has to start somewhere!

2 Work in pairs. Look at your storyboard again. Pick out some e-tivities; grasp the green sticky note in your hand. You might like to start with easier ones, for example, those that use text, words and websites already available.

3 Then agree between you who will start to design which e-tivity—try to tackle different parts of the scaffold, unit, module or programme so you'll have something for the reality checkers (who come next) to get their teeth into.

4 Take one e-tivity per pair or group and draft it out on paper using the invitation on page 3.

5 When you have an e-tivity that you think may work, move to the computer which has been pre-prepared with your LMS/VLE or whatever platform you are using. Each pair builds one e-tivity directly online in the LMS/VLE, returning to the storyboard to adjust as necessary. Put as much as you can in but do it fairly quickly. Put links to URLs for sparks if possible.

6 Insert a clear marker in the LMS/VLE page (such as a holding image or coloured alert text) where you need to return later or ask for further technical help—for example, to insert an interactive diagram.

7 As soon as an e-tivity looks usable, move on to another one.

Stage 4: Check reality

Ask your students, colleagues, peers and managers to come and help you for an hour or two. They will be your critical friends. It's useful if people know something about the topic but they do not need to be experts.

Ensure that by the time the reality checkers arrive (plan for around lunchtime on day 2—food seems to help) you have some e-tivities ready for them to try out. Depending on how many e-tivities you have designed, you may need to allow up to an hour. Ask the reality checkers to make notes on a form that provides some basic guidance and that they can leave with you (see Resources for Practitioners 24).

Sit out of their way, but be available in case they need technical help. Do not interrupt or intervene unless they faint. If they ask for help, offer enough to get them started again. Do not enter into explanations, but encourage them to work online and autonomously as much as possible.

It's a good time for the Carpe Diem team to take time out, eat their lunch and return to discussing any contentious issues or reflect and review on what they have learned, while the reality checking is going on.

Then ask the reality checkers to give direct feedback to the team based on their experience of trying out the e-tivities. Ask your reality checkers to go through the e-tivities and explain and summarize their reactions to you. Ask them questions by all means—but try and listen and not get defensive. (Really—you'll have a chance to evaluate soon!) Ask them to leave their notes with you.

Say thanks very nicely.

The reality checkers have left the building.

Stage 5: Review and adjust

As a team, list your reality checkers' main concerns and suggestions. Talk through the impact of these comments. Decide whether you need to:

- rethink any of the components of your blueprint;
- adjust your storyboard—especially considering navigation, timings and assessment;
- work on immediate improvements to the e-tivities;
- plan the next steps.

Before you move on, just make sure you are in a different and better place with your course than when you started (if not, why not?) on the morning of day 1.

Stage 6: Planning your next steps

You need another big flip chart or white board (or wiki or Google Docs) divided addressing:

- What else needs doing and who will do it?
- Assessment of the risks (how are you going to find the time to complete the work, what might interfere, who else might need to be involved).
- What other resources or people you need to consult, acquire or include, as well as resources that you had available but did not use.
- Clear deadlines.
- A date for your next team meeting when you will review progress.

- What post-Carpe Diem follow-up would be useful? For example, identifying and training your e-moderators (please!).

Now build an action plan for completing your online unit. You can do this on a wiki, Google Docs or whatever, but we find a big physical poster on the wall works well too.

Follow-up two to four weeks later

- Check progress on the action plan; especially consider timescales and deadlines.
- Plan further actions not originally thought of—don't forget addressing quality learning issues and plans to disseminate your achievements.
- Discuss any problems with the storyboard and technology availability, revise e-tivities and develop new ones and discuss other design issues.
- Make sure you have sufficient technology support to help implement the design.
- Consider a short e-moderating online course to develop delivery skills (details at atimod.com).
- Share what you've learned from each other, decide who else to tell . . . celebrate.

This resource is based on the original Carpe Diem model process developed by Professor Gilly Salmon, with input from teams at the Caledonian Business School. The model was tested and refined at the University of Bournemouth and Anglia Ruskin University, and further developed by the ADELIE, ADDER, CHEETAH and DUCKLING projects and by Dr Alejandro Armellini and Beyond Distance teams at the University of Leicester, by the Australian Digital Futures Institute at University of Southern Queensland and by Learning Transformations Teams at Swinburne University of Technology, Melbourne, Australia.

Resources for practitioners 22

Becoming a Carpe Diem facilitator

In recent years I've been running short Carpe Diem facilitator training sessions. Here are the qualities and knowledge you'd need to acquire, or help others to, if you'd like to trial Carpe Diems beyond a prototype. If you feel they add value to your redesign and transformation agendas, then why not run some training sessions?

1 **Excellent facilitation skills**—look for people with really good facilitation skills. These are acquired over time and practice, online or offline.
2 Completion of **an e-moderating development programme**. Becoming and practising as an online e-moderator helps a great deal in understanding how good simple design transforms not only the participants' learning experiences but that of staff too.
3 A good understanding of **designing for learning, delivering for participation**. There are people around who are good at seeing the bigger picture in learning design, but they may not have labelled their skills in that way.
4 **Learning technology appreciation and enthusiasm**—I don't mean highly technical knowledge, but instead the ability to make good choices for e-tivities sparks and participation (see Chapter 4).
5 Good understanding of **low-cost; high-value for learning technologies**. If you think the way to do great e-learning is to set up extensive

and expensive 'content' and development, Carpe Diem and e-tivities are not for you! It's to do with recognizing and helping others do a great job with what's around, as quickly as possible.

6   Good understanding of the **five-stage model and how to apply it**. People who are convinced about the strong need to pace and provide a good process for online and blended learning—what we call a 'scaffold'. The five-stage model is well rehearsed and easy to use—if you don't like it or it doesn't meet your needs, find another one, *but have one!*

7   Good understanding of **e-tivities design** and how to use them. Try it for yourself before developing others.

8   Understanding of **Open Educational Resources and Creative Commons licences**. This is appreciation that online is *not* about 'writing' courses (so twentieth-century!) and what online resources can be legally and productively used instead (see Resources for Practitioners 3).

9   Understanding of the power of Carpe Diems as **a transformational approach** to bring a whole course, department, institution or country (OK . . . maybe not country) into a digital world. People who really want to make a difference to the new world of learning . . .

Resources for practitioners 23

The Carpe Diem
planning process

Carpe Diem planning process

	Carpe Diem	Environment	Structure	Purposes	Timing
1	**Essential:** Pre-meeting	Face-to-face or online	Discussion	● Clarification of Carpe Diem's purpose and scope. ● Student evaluation of previous learning, if relevant. ● Presentation of pedagogical problems and challenges. ● Expectations management. ● Preparation. ● Motivation and engagement.	1 to 1.5 hours, around 2–4 weeks prior to main 2-day workshop
2	**Optional:** Good for those with no experience of designing or delivering online	Online	Two practice e-tivities —e.g. working together in an online environment and then a course resource audit task with a wiki	● Introduce team to e-tivities in a collaborative environment. ● Provide examples of e-tivities, with e-moderation, right from the start. ● Introduce teams to open and collaborative knowledge practices. ● Save time at the main workshop.	Introduced at pre-meeting or before; maximum 2.5 hours per Carpe Diem participant
3	**Optional:** Involve the Carpe Diem design team in an e-moderation course	Online	Use the LMS and other possible technology platforms	● Gain experience of understanding learning and working online. ● Gain experience of the technologies in practice. ● Model the five-stage model and the structure of e-tivities.	Any time

#		Format		Details	Timing
4	**Essential:** Main workshop 2-day Carpe Diem	Face-to-face, online or blended	The six stages	• Generate the key Carpe Diem deliverables: blueprint, storyboard, running and tested e-tivities with action plan.	2 full days
5	**Optional:** Post-workshop consolidation	Online	The Carpe Diem workshop team or others to trial the one or two of the newly designed e-tivities	• Progress, consolidate and refine the work already done, e.g. trial, reflect on, review and improve e-tivities already produced. Check progress against Action Plan.	Introduced at the main workshop; around 2.5 hours per participant
6	**Essential:** Post-workshop meeting	Face-to-face	Review of progress against the action plan	• Keep focus on design and development against the action plan, in preparation for delivery. • Identify further support needs and how to meet them. • Review and celebrate the course in its final draft format.	2 to 3 hours, approximately 4 weeks after main workshop
7	**Essential:** Run the newly designed course with 6 to 6,000 participants.	Online, or with blend	Set up feedback from the participants	• Check out what works well, what adds value. • Plan any changes (there will be some), but you may find that small changes, e.g. to a resource or simplifying invitation instructions, make a big difference. • Start building a community of e-tivities practice from your e-moderators.	As soon as possible; 2 weeks from the Carpe Diem main workshop is the fastest so far!

Adapted from planners in use by Professor Ale Armellini at University of Northampton and in the Learning Transformations Unit at Swinburne University of Technology, with thanks.

Resources for practitioners 24

Reality checkers' feedback

We are trying to design a highly engaging course quickly. We appreciate your time and feedback in helping us to make our course the 'best ever'. You need to complete the tasks, but please try and approach them as if you were a participant.

Please tell us the good and bad news, but if possible in a way we can action quickly.

E-tivity number or name:

Your first impressions and/or reactions. Would you want to take part?

Is it clear what you are supposed to do? Note any suggested improvements:

Would you find this e-tivities motivating and/or interesting? Why?

Can you identify anything you might learn or gain from undertaking this e-tivity?

How might the e-tivity be improved for you?

Any other comments?

References

Armellini, A., and Jones, S. (2008). Carpe Diem: Seizing each day to foster change in e-learning design. *Reflecting Education* 4(1), 17–29.

Armellini, A., Jones, S., and Salmon, G. (2007). Developing assessment for learning through e-tivities. *Proceedings of the 11th International Computer-Assisted Assessment Conference* (pp.13–17). Loughborough: Loughborough University. Retrieved December 8, 2012, from: http://caaconference.co.uk/pastConferences/2007/proceedings/Armellini%20A%20Jones%20S%20Salmon%20G%20b3_formatted.pdf.

Armellini, A., Salmon, G., and Hawkridge, D. (2009). The Carpe Diem journey: Designing for learning and transformation. In T. Mayes, D. Morrison, H. Mellar, P. Bullen, and M. Oliver (Eds.), *Transforming Higher Education Through Technology-Enhanced Learning*. York: The Higher Education Academy.

Ash, C., and Bacsich, P. (2002). The costs of networked learning. In C. Steeples and C. Jones (Eds.), *Networked learning: Perspectives and issues*. London: Springer-Verlag.

Belbin, R.M. (1981). *Management teams: Why they succeed or fail*. Oxford: Butterworth Heinemann.

Biggs, J.B., and Tang, C. (2011). *Teaching for quality learning at university* (4th ed.). Berkshire: Open University Press.

Bird, A., and Osland, J.S. (2005). Making sense of intercultural collaboration. *International Studies of Management and Organization*, 35(4), 115–132.

Bonk, C. (2009). *The world is open: How web technology is revolutionising education*. San Francisco, CA: Jossey-Bass.

Bonk, C.J., and Zhang, K. (2008). *Empowering online learning: 100+ activities for reading, reflecting, displaying, and doing.* San Francisco: Jossey-Bass.

Boulton, H., and Hramiak, A. (2012). E-flection: The development of reflective communities of learning for trainee teachers through the use of shared online web logs. *Reflective Practice, 13*(4), 503–515. doi:10.1080/14623943.2012.670619.

Carmel, E., and Espinosa, J.A. (2011). *I'm working while they're sleeping: Time zone separation, challenges and solutions.* USA: Nedder Stream Press.

Conole, G. (2012). *Designing for learning in an open world.* New York: Springer.

Coombs, N. (2010). *Making online teaching accessible: Inclusive course design for students with disabilities.* San Francisco: Jossey-Bass.

Covey, S.R. (2004). *Seven habits of highly effective people: Powerful lessons in personal change.* New York: Free Press.

Crosta, L., and McConnell, D. (2008, May). *Online learning groups' development: A grounded international comparison.* Paper presented at the 6th Annual International Conference Networked Learning, Halkidiki, Greece. Retrieved November 7, 2012, from: www.networkedlearningconference.org.uk/past/nlc2008/abstracts/PDFs/Crosta_61–68.pdf.

Crystal, D. (2004). *A glossary of netspeak and textspeak.* Edinburgh: Edinburgh University Press.

Crystal, D. (2008). *Txtng: The gr8 db8.* New York: Oxford University Press.

Csikszentmihalyi, M. (2002). *Flow: The classic work on how to achieve happiness* (2nd ed.). London: Random House.

de Andres Martinez, C. (2012). Developing metacognition at a distance: Sharing students' learning strategies on a reflective blog. *Computer Assisted Language Learning, 25*(2), 199–212.

Dirckinck-Holmfeld, L., Hodgson, V., and McConnell, D. (Eds.) (2012). *Exploring the theory, pedagogy and practice of networked learning.* New York: Springer.

Eden, C. (2004). Analyzing cognitive maps to help structure issues or problems. *European Journal of Operational Research, 159*(3), 673–686.

Ehrmann, S.C. (2012). Why faculty resist. *Distance Learning, 9*(2), 60–64.

Ellis, R.A., and Goodyear, P. (2010). *Students' experiences of e-learning in higher education: The ecology of sustainable innovation.* London and New York: Routledge.

Flavin, M. (2012). Disruptive technologies in higher education. *Research in Learning Technology, 20,* 102–111. Retrieved November 12, 2012, from: http://dx.doi.org/10.3402/rlt.v20i0.19184.

Forte, J., Gomes, D., Gondim, C., and de Almeida, C. (2011). Educational services in Second Life: A study based on flow theory. *International Journal of Web-Based Learning and Teaching Technologies, 6*(2), 1–17. doi:10.4018/jwltt.2011040101.

Friesen, N. (2011). *The place of the classroom and the space of the screen: New literacies and digital epistemologies*. New York: Peter Lang.

Ghani, J.A., and Deshpande, S.P. (1994). Task characteristics and the experience of optimal flow in human–computer interaction. *Journal of Psychology, 128*(4), 381.

Goleman, D. (2011). *The brain and emotional intelligence: New insights* [Kindle edition]. Northampton, MA: More Than Sound LLC.

Goodfellow, R., and Lamy, M.N. (2009). *Learning cultures in online education*. New York: Continuum Studies in Education.

Grossman, D. (2002). *Be my knife*. London: Bloomsbury.

Gunawardena, C.N., Hermans, M., Sanchez, D., Richmond, C., Bohley, M., and Tuttle, R. (2009). A theoretical framework for building online communities of practice with social networking tools. *Educational Media International, 46*(1), 3–16. doi:10.1080/09523980802588626.

Herrington, J., Reeves, T.C., and Oliver, R. (2010). *A guide to authentic e-learning*. New York: Routledge.

Hodgson, V.E. (2008). Learning spaces, context and auto/biography in online learning communities. *International Journal of Web Based Communities, 4*(2), 9. doi:10.1504/IJWBC.2008.017670.

Holley, K.A., and Taylor, B.J. (2009). Undergraduate student socialization and learning in an online professional curriculum. *Innovative Higher Education, 33*(4), 257–269. doi:10.1007/s10755–008–9083–y.

Jaques, D., and Salmon, G. (2008). *Learning in groups: A handbook for face-to-face and online environments* (4th ed.). London and New York: Routledge.

Jewitt, C. (2008). *Technology, literacy, learning: A multimodal approach*. Abingdon: Routledge.

Joint Information Systems Committee (2012). *Plagiarism*. Retrieved September 30, 2012, from: http://www.jisc.ac.uk/whatwedo/topics/plagiarism.aspx.

Jones, J., Gaffney-Rhys, R., and Jones, E. (2011). Social network sites and student–lecturer communication: An academic voice. *Journal of Further and Higher Education, 35*(2), 201–219.

Kearney, M., Shuck, S., Burden, K., and Aubusson, P. (2012). Viewing mobile learning from a pedagogical perspective. *Research in Learning Technology, 20*(1), 37–53.

Kirkpatrick, D., and Kirkpatrick, J. (2005). *Transferring learning to behaviour: Using the four levels to improve performance*. San Francisco: Berrett-Koehler.

Lauzon, A. (2000). Situating cognition and crossing borders: Resisting the hegemony of mediated education. *British Journal of Educational Technology, 30*(3), 261–276.

Laurillard, D. (2012). *Teaching as a design science*. NY and London: Routledge.

Lawrence, L., and Gammon, S. (2004). Reflections on a pedagogic research project: Applying flow theory in an educational setting. *LSA Newsletter, 69*, 27–35.

Littlejohn, A., and Pegler, C. (2007). *Preparing for blended e-learning.* Abingdon and New York: Routledge.

MacGilchrist, B., Myers, K., and Reed, J. (2004). *The intelligent school* (2nd ed.). London: Sage.

Malone, E. (2004). Seize the day: Developing e-learning content. *Library and Information Update, 3*(9), 36–37.

McClelland, D.C. (1985). *Human motivation.* New York: Cambridge University Press.

McConnell, D. (2006). *E-learning groups and communities of practice.* Berkshire: Open University Press.

McDermott, R. (1999). Why information technology inspired but cannot deliver knowledge management. *California Management Review, 41*(4), 103–117.

Meyer, J., and Land, R. (2005). Threshold concepts and troublesome knowledge (2): Epistemological considerations and a conceptual framework for teaching and learning. *Higher Education, 49*(3), 373–388. doi:10.1007/s10734–004–6779–5.

Moon, J.A. (2006). *Learning journals: A handbook for reflective practice and Professional Development.* Abingdon: Routledge.

Morgan, G. (2006). *Images of organization* (updated ed.). London: Sage.

Murray, J.H. (1997). *Hamlet on the holodeck: The future of narrative in cyberspace.* New York: The Free Press.

Oblinger, D.G. (2012). IT as a game changer. In D.G. Oblinger (ed.), *Game changers: education and information technologies* (pp. 37–52). Retrieved December 8, 2012, from: http://net.educause.edu/ir/library/pdf/pub72033.pdf.

Osland, J.S., Bird, A., and Mendenall, M. (2012). Developing global mindsets and global leadership capabilities. In G.K. Stahl, I. Björkman, and S. Morris (Eds.), *Handbook of research in international human resources management* (2nd ed., pp. 220–252). Cheltenham: Edward Elgar Publishing Limited.

Parry, M. (2012). History harvest may spawn a new kind of MOOC. *Chronicle of Higher Education,* 29 December. Retrieved December 30, 2012, from: http://chronicle.com/blogs/wiredcampus/history-harvest-project-may-spawn-a-new-kind-of-mooc/41329.

Pea, R. (2004). The social and technological dimensions of scaffolding and related theoretical concepts for learning, education and human activity. *Journal of the Learning Sciences, 13*(1), 423–451.

Preece, J., and Shneiderman, B. (2009). The reader-to-leader framework: Motivating technology-mediated social participation. *AIS Transactions on Human–Computer Interaction, 1*(1), 13–32.

Reilly, J., Gallagher-Lepak, S., and Killion, C. (2012). 'Me and my computer': Emotional factors in online learning. *Nursing Education Perspectives, 33*(2), 100–105.

Ross, J. (2012). Just what is being reflected in online reflection? New literacies for new media learning practices. In L. Dirckinck-Holmfeld, V. Hodgson, and D. McConnell (Eds.), *Exploring the theory, pedagogy and practice of networked learning* (pp. 191–207). New York: Springer.

Rumble, G. (2010). Flexing costs and reflecting on methods. In E. Burge, C. Gibson, and T. Gibson (Eds.), *Flexibility in higher education: Promises, ambiguities, challenges* (pp. 264–301). Athabasca, Alberta: Athabasca University Press.

Sailers, E. (2009). *iPhone, iPad and iPod Touch apps for (special) education.* Retrieved August 1, 2012, from: http://theumbrellanetwork.org/wp-content/uploads/2011/04/iPhone-iPad-and-iPod-touch-Apps-AUS1.pdf.

Salmon, G. (2002a). Approaches to researching teaching and learning online. In C. Steeples and C. Jones (Eds.), *Networked learning: Perspectives and issues.* London: Springer-Verlag.

Salmon, G. (2002b). *E-tivities: The key to active online learning.* London and New York: Routledge.

Salmon, G. (2002c). Mirror, mirror, on my screen . . . : Exploring online reflections. *British Journal of Educational Technology, 33*(4), 383–396.

Salmon, G. (2003). *Anytime this century: An exploration of achieving more with less for implementing e-learning.* Paper presented at Strategic Responses to Change, Cambridge. Retrieved December 8, 2012, from: www.atimod.com/research/presentations/JISCcambsoct2003gilly.ppt.

Salmon, G. (2009). The future for (Second) Life and learning. *British Journal of Educational Technology, 40*(3), 526–538. doi:10.1111/j.1467–8535.2009.00967.x.

Salmon, G. (2011). *E-moderating: The key to teaching and learning online* (3rd ed.). New York: Routledge.

Salmon, G., and Edirisingha, P. (Eds.) (2008). *Podcasting for learning in universities.* Berkshire: Open University Press and McGraw-Hill.

Salmon, G., Jones, S., and Armellini, A. (2008). Building institutional capability in e-learning design. *ALT-J: Research in Learning Technology, 16*(2), 95–109. doi: 10.1080/09687760802315978.

Salmon, G., Nie, M., and Edirisingha, P. (2010). Developing a five-stage model of learning in 'Second Life'. *Educational Research, 52*(2), 169–182. doi: 10.1080/00131881.2010.482744.

Savin-Baden, M., and Wilkie, K. (Eds.) (2006). *Problem-based learning online.* New York: Open University Press.

Scharmer, C.O. (2009). *Theory U: Leading from the future as it emerges.* San Francisco, CA: Berrett-Koehler Publishers Inc.

Schön, D. (1983). *The reflective practitioner.* New York: Basic Books.

Sharpe, R., Beetham, H., and De Freitas, S.D. (Eds) (2010). *Rethinking learning for a digital age: How learners are shaping their own experiences.* London and New York: Routledge.

Siddiqui, N., and Roberts, G. (2004, April). *Electronic marketing online: Reflections and future developments*. Paper presented at the BEST Conference: Reflections on Teaching: The Impact of Learning, Edinburgh.

Spectronics. (2012). *Apps for special education*. Retrieved August 1, 2012, from: http://www.spectronicsinoz.com/apps-for-special-education.

Stefani, L., Mason, R., and Pegler, C. (2007). *The educational potential of e-portfolios*. London and New York: Routledge.

Sternberg, R.J. (2010). *College admissions for the 21st century*. Cambridge, MA: Harvard University Press.

Tolmie, A., and Boyle, A. (2000). Factors influencing the success of computer-mediated communication (CMC) environments in university teaching: A review and a case study. *Computers and Education, 34*(2), 119–140. doi:10.1016/S0360–1315(00)00008–7.

Tuckman, B.W. (1965). Developmental sequence in small groups. *Psychological Bulletin, 63*(6), 384–399. doi:10.1037/h0022100.

Tuckman, B.W., and Jensen, M.C. (1977). Stages of small-group development revisited. *Group and Organization Studies, 2*(4), 419–427.

Wenger, E. (2000). Communities of practice and social learning systems. *Organization, 7*(2), 225–246.

Wenger, E. (2006). *Communities of practice: A brief introduction*. Retrieved August 9, 2012, from: http://www.ewenger.com/theory/index.htm.

Wenger, E., White, N., and Smith, J.D. (2009). *Digital habitats: Stewarding technology for communities*. Portland, OR: CPsquare.

Williams, S., Watkins, K., Daley, B., Courtenay, B., Davis, M., and Dymock, D. (2001). Facilitating cross-cultural online discussion groups: Implications for practice. *Distance Education, 22*(1), 151–167.

Yu-Chih, H., Backman, S.J., and Backman, K.F. (2010). Student attitude toward virtual learning in Second Life: A flow theory approach. *Journal of Teaching in Travel and Tourism, 10*(4), 312–334. doi:10.1080/15313220.2010.525425.

Index